MW01244207

To: Cookbook Enthusiasts

Farm families have been the backbone of this country for generations, so it is with a lot of pride that we offer this collection of "Recipes From America's Farm Kitchens."

We want to express our appreciation to every person who sent us a recipe from across rural America. We hope you enjoy them all . . . and keep listening to AgriTalk.

Mark Perrin, President

Cathy Perrin, Cookbook Editor

P.S. To help ensure we have professionals devoted to reporting information to America's farmers, we are pleased to make a donation to the National Association of Farm Broadcasters Scholarship for each cookbook purchased.

Published and Printed By
Cookbook Publishers, Inc.
P.O. Box 15920
Lenexa, Kansas 66285-5920

THIS BOOK includes the finest plastic ring binders available, BUT, like most plastics, the BINDERS CAN BE DAMAGED BY EXCESSIVE HEAT, so AVOID exposing them to the direct rays of the SUN, or excessive heat such as IN A CAR on a hot day, or on the top of the kitchen STOVE. If not exposed to heat, the binders will last indefinitely.

My mother taught me to clean my plate . . . and I have held true to her teachings ever since.

I love good food, and none has ever been prepared with such care and quality as that from America's farm kitchens. I have spent many years in agricultural broadcasting and have spoken after dinner at hundreds of meetings. Those events which had a "covered dish dinner" were my favorites, because I knew that the premiere dishes of the rural homemakers and farm wives would be served.

This cookbook is full of the best recipes from the best cooks in the country. I hope that you can enjoy them all in the coming years and if you are a person who has been transplanted to rural America and get invited to bring a "favorite covered dish" to supper, just turn through these pages until you find one that suits you and claim it as your own!

The staff and guests of Agritalk have included some of our favorite recipes. Dr. Val Farmer provides a recipe to A Banquet for Life and Mark Vail our executive producer cites the ingredients to Blueberry-Stuffed "French Toast."

I, on the other hand, feel that the recipe for a good life and good health is good food.

If you feel that you have a need to diet . . . just put my picture on the front of your refrigerator and that should turn you away from the calories for a few days.

Let your friends know about this recipe book (an order form is in the back) and by all means let them in on Agritalk!

Here's to America's farmers and the abundance of high quality foods that their labor provides.

Ken Root

TABLE OF CONTENTS

FAVORITE RECIPES
FROM MY COOKBOOK

Recipe Name	Page Number

Appetizers, Beverages

FOOD QUANTITIES FOR 25, 50, AND 100 SERVINGS

FOOD	25 SERVINGS	50 SERVINGS	100 SERVINGS
Rolls	4 doz.	8 doz.	16 doz.
Bread	50 slices or 3 1-lb. loaves	100 slices or 6 1-lb. loaves	200 slices or 12 1-lb. loaves
Butter	½ pound	¾ to 1 pound	1½ pounds
Mayonnaise	1 cup	2 to 3 cups	4 to 6 cups
Mixed Filling for Sandwiches (meat, eggs, fish)	1½ quarts	2½ to 3 quarts	5 to 6 quarts
Mixed Filling (sweet-fruit)	1 quart	1¾ to 2 quarts	2½ to 4 quarts
Jams & Preserves	1½ lb.	3 lb.	6 lb.
Crackers	1½ lb.	3 lb.	6 lb.
Cheese (2 oz. per serving)	3 lb.	6 lb.	12 lb.
Soup	1½ gal.	3 gal.	6 gal.
Salad Dressings	1 pt.	2½ pt.	½ gal.
Meat, Poultry or Fish:			
Wieners (beef)	6½ pounds	13 pounds	25 pounds
Hamburger	9 pounds	18 pounds	35 pounds
Turkey or chicken	13 pounds	25 to 35 pounds	50 to 75 pounds
Fish, large whole (round)	13 pounds	25 pounds	50 pounds
Fish, fillets or steaks	7½ pounds	15 pounds	30 pounds
Salads, Casseroles, Vegetables:			
Potato Salad	4¼ quarts	2¼ gallons	4½ gallons
Scalloped Potatoes	4½ quarts or 1 12x20" pan	8½ quarts	17 quarts
Mashed Potatoes	9 lb.	18-20 lb.	25-35 lb.
Spaghetti	1¼ gallons	2½ gallons	5 gallons
Baked Beans	¾ gallon	1¼ gallons	2½ gallons
Jello Salad	¾ gallon	1¼ gallons	2½ gallons
Canned Vegetables	1 #10 can	2½ #10 cans	4 #10 cans
Fresh Vegetables:			
Lettuce (for salads)	4 heads	8 heads	15 heads
Carrots (3 oz. or ½ c.)	6¼ lb.	12½ lb.	25 lb.
Tomatoes	3-5 lb.	7-10 lb.	14-20 lb.
Desserts:			
Watermelon	37½ pounds	75 pounds	150 pounds
Fruit Cup (½ c. per serving)	3 qt.	6 qt.	12 qt.
Cake	1 10x12" sheet cake / 1½ 10" layer cakes	1 12x20" sheet cake / 3 10" layer cakes	2 12x20" sheet cakes / 6 10" layer cakes
Whipping Cream	¾ pint	1½ to 2 pints	3 pints
Ice Cream:			
Brick	3¼ quarts	6½ quarts	12½ quarts
Bulk	2¼ quarts	4½ quarts or 1¼ gallons	9 quarts or 2½ gallons
Beverages:			
Coffee	½ pound and 1½ gal. water	1 pound and 3 gal. water	2 pounds and 6 gal. water
Tea	1/12 pound and 1½ gal. water	1/6 pound and 3 gal. water	1/3 pound and 6 gal. water
Lemonade	10 to 15 lemons, 1½ gal. water	20 to 30 lemons, 3 gal. water	40 to 60 lemons, 6 gal. water

APPETIZERS, BEVERAGES

BLACK-EYED PEA DIP

1 can chili (no beans)
1 can black-eyed peas, drained
1 lb. Velveeta mild Mexican cheese,
    cubed

1 onion, chopped

Mix all ingredients. Bake at 350° for approximately 30 minutes; stir during baking. Serve with Fritos.

Ken and Gail Root, AgriTalk

MOLDED AVOCADO PINWHEEL

Delight your guests with this impressive spread.

1 env. unflavored gelatin
1/4 c. cold water
1 c. mashed avocados (2 to 3
    avocados)
1 Tbsp. lemon juice
1 (6 oz.) pkg. Italian salad dressing
    mix
1 pt. dairy sour cream (2 c.)
3 Tbsp. chopped parsley
Dash of Tabasco sauce

2 or 3 drops of green food coloring
    (if desired)
Bread rounds or crackers
Assorted garnishes (such as cooked
    baby shrimp, chopped green
    onions, chopped cucumbers,
    chopped ripe olives, red or
    black caviar, chopped tomatoes,
    or a tomato rose)

Oil a 9½ inch porcelain quiche dish, glass pie dish or a flan tin with indented bottom. In a small saucepan, sprinkle gelatin over cold water. Let stand 5 minutes to soften. Cook over medium heat until mixture just comes to a boil and gelatin is dissolved. In a large bowl or food processor fitted with the metal blade, blend avocados, lemon juice, salad dressing mix, sour cream, parsley, and Tabasco sauce. Add dissolved gelatin. Mix thoroughly. Stir in 2 or 3 drops of green food coloring if desired. Pour mixture into prepared mold. Cover with plastic wrap. Refrigerate until firm. May be refrigerated up to 2 days. Do not freeze.

If using a quiche dish or pie dish, it is not necessary to unmold spread. If using a flan tin, unmold before serving. Run the tip of a table knife around the edges, dip bottom of mold in warm water, and invert onto platter. Decorate with 4 or 5 suggested garnishes. Serve with bread rounds or crackers. Makes 3 cups.

Rhonda Stevenson, AgriTalk

FILLER-UP CHICKEN SUNFLOWER SPREAD

2 c. cooked cubed chicken
2 stalks celery
1/4 lb. cubed Colby or Cheddar
    cheese
1/2 c. sunflower kernel, salted and
    roasted

Salad dressing
1/2 tsp. celery salt
1/2 tsp. onion salt
1/8 tsp. coarse ground pepper

In a food processor or by hand, chop the chicken, celery, cheese, and the sunflower kernel. Be careful not to chop too fine. Mix with enough salad dressing to the desired consistency. Blend in celery salt, onion salt, pepper, and salad seasoning. Use this filling in sandwiches, pita bread, crepes, and crackers or shape into a ball and chill for an appetizer roll.

Reprinted with permission from the National Sunflower Association.

Ann Schwartz, North Dakota

MEATBALLS

1½ lb. ground beef
2 eggs
⅓ c. onion, minced

Sauce (about ½ cup - recipe
    follows)
Crushed crackers

Sauce:

2 c. ketchup
1½ c. brown sugar (do not pack
    cup)

2 tsp. garlic powder
2 tsp. liquid smoke

Mix beef, eggs, onion, and sauce together. Add enough crackers to form 1½ inch balls. Place raw meatballs in an *ungreased* cake pan. Spoon remaining sauce over meatballs. Place *uncovered* cake pan into oven at 350° for 50 to 60 minutes. Scoop balls onto platter to cool.

May use sauce on anything imaginable (chicken, pork chops, sandwiches, etc.).

Susan Reul, Illinois

MOM'S SNACK

1 slice white bread
Soft butter

Sugar
Cinnamon (optional)

Sprinkle sugar on top of buttered white bread.

Rustin Hamilton, AgriTalk

SUNFLOWER CHEESE SPREAD

1 tsp. minced onion
1 Tbsp. dry sherry
8 oz. cream cheese
2 Tbsp. mayonnaise

3 oz. smoked sliced beef
¼ c. chopped stuffed olives
1 Tbsp. chopped sunflower kernel,
    roasted and salted

Mix onion and sherry. Set aside. Combine cream cheese and mayonnaise. Add onion mixture. Snip or cut beef into fine pieces. Add beef, cheese, and olives to cheese mixture. Stir in sunflower kernel. Chill for several hours.

Sunflower kernels contain *twice* as much iron as raisins and *three times* as much as peanuts!

Reprinted with permission from the National Sunflower Association.

Pat Beck, North Dakota

CHEESY SUN CRISPS

2 c. (8 oz.) shredded Cheddar
    cheese
½ c. grated Parmesan cheese
½ c. softened sunflower margarine
3 Tbsp. water

1 c. all-purpose flour
¼ tsp. salt (optional)
1 c. quick-cooking oats
⅔ c. roasted, salted sunflower
    kernels

Beat cheeses, margarine, and water until well blended; add flour and salt. Mix well. Stir in oats and sunflower kernels, mixing until thoroughly blended. Shape dough into 12 inch long roll; wrap securely. Refrigerate about 4 hours. (Dough may be stored up to a week in refrigerator.) Cut into ⅛ to ¼ inch slices; flatten slightly. Bake on lightly greased cookie sheet in preheated 400° oven for 8 to 10 minutes until edges are light golden brown. Remove from pan at once; cool on wire rack.

Reprinted with permission from the National Sunflower Association.
Mrs. Orlene Sheldon, North Dakota

HAM AND CHEESE BALL

2 (4½ oz.) cans deviled ham
1 (8 oz.) cream cheese, softened
1 (4 oz.) pkg. dry Ranch style
    dressing mix

½ c. tomato, diced
½ c. green pepper, diced (optional)
2 c. shredded mild Cheddar cheese

In medium bowl, combine all ingredients. Refrigerate until firm enough to handle. Form into a ball and roll in chopped pecans or parsley. Refrigerate till ready to use.

Bea Taylor, Iowa

TORTILLA PINWHEELS

8 oz. cream cheese, softened
8 oz. sour cream
4 oz. green chilies, well drained
4 oz. can chopped black olives, well
    drained

1 c. grated Cheddar cheese
½ pkg. taco seasoning mix
1 to 2 Tbsp. chopped green onion

Mix preceding ingredients; divide and spread over 5 (10 inch) tortillas (or 1 small package). Roll up; wrap in plastic wrap and twist the ends. Refrigerate several hours. Slice into ½ to ¾ inch pieces. Serve with taco sauce for dipping.

Linda Marek, Iowa

GOOD SNACK

1½ c. sugar
1 c. butter

½ c. corn syrup

Add 1 teaspoon vanilla.

Pour over:

5 c. Crispix
3 c. corn flakes

3 c. small pretzels
2 c. mixed nuts

Put on cookie sheet and let dry.

Brenda Kovar, Minnesota

SUNNY DIP

1 (8 oz.) pkg. cream cheese
¼ c. milk
¼ c. chopped onion
¼ c. chopped celery

¼ c. chopped sweet pickle
¼ c. sunflower kernel, roasted and
   salted

Blend softened cream cheese and milk. Add chopped vegetables, pickles, and sunflower kernel. Mix until just blended. Use as a dip for fresh vegetables, chips, and crackers.

Reprinted with permission from the National Sunflower Association.

Donna Stillwell, North Dakota

SHRIMP BUTTER

½ lb. Land O' Lakes sweet cream
   butter, softened
¼ c. mayonnaise
1 (8 oz.) pkg. cream cheese,
   softened

¼ c. finely chopped onions
1 (4¼ oz.) can tiny shrimp, rinsed,
   drained, and broken
1 Tbsp. lemon juice

In small mixer bowl, beat butter first. Add cream cheese; beat and then add mayonnaise. Beat at medium speed, scraping bowl often, until light and fluffy (2 to 3 minutes). Add remaining ingredients; continue beating until well mixed (1 to 2 minutes). Serve with crackers. Store refrigerated. Yield: 2 cups.

Mary Ann Cappo, Kansas

HOT SPINACH DIP

1 (10 oz.) frozen spinach, thawed
   and well drained
½ lb. cooked ham, diced
4 oz. shredded fat free Mozzarella
   cheese
½ c. fat free sour cream
3 oz. fat free cream cheese,
   softened

¼ c. chopped green onions
1 Tbsp. horseradish
1 fresh jalapeno pepper, seeded and
   minced
1 tsp. salt
½ tsp. pepper

Combine ingredients in a large bowl. Spread in a 9 inch pie pan that you have sprayed with Pam. Cook 15 minutes at 375°. Garnish with sour cream and green onions.

Debi Hensley, Kansas

TEX-MEX DIP

Layer 1: Spread 2 cans bean dip.

Layer 2 - Mix:

3 mashed avocados
2 tsp. lemon juice

½ tsp. salt
¼ tsp. pepper

Layer over bean dip.

Layer 3:

1 c. mayonnaise
1 pkg. taco mix

8 oz. sour cream

Mix together and spread over Layer 2.

Layer 4: Sprinkle 1 bunch sliced green onions.

Layer 5: Spread 6 ounce can pitted and sliced black olives.

Layer 6: Layer 3 medium cut up tomatoes.

Layer 7: Sprinkle 8 ounces shredded cheese.

Layer in 9x13 inch pan. Serve with tortilla chips.

Laura Montgomery, Texas

ROLL-UP SNACKS

24 slices white sandwich bread (cut off crusts)
8 oz. softened cream cheese
1 c. sugar

1 egg yolk
3 or 4 sticks oleo
Cinnamon

Mix cream cheese, sugar, and egg yolk with mixer. Melt 1 stick of oleo at a time. Cool slightly. Spread cheese mixture on each slice of bread. Roll each up like a jelly roll. Dip in melted oleo and then roll in mixture of 1 cup sugar and 1 teaspoon cinnamon. Put on cookie sheet and freeze. Bake in 350° oven for 15 to 20 minutes. *Do not thaw before baking.*

Delicious. Can cut in half to serve.

Ruth Kenaley, Iowa

SNACK MIX

1½ c. Corn Chex cereal
1½ c. Rice Chex cereal
1 c. Cheerios
2 c. pretzel sticks
1 c. dry roasted peanuts

6 Tbsp. margarine, melted
1 Tbsp. Worcestershire sauce
½ tsp. celery salt
½ tsp. garlic salt

In large bowl, combine Rice and Corn Chex, Cheerios, peanuts, and pretzel sticks. Combine melted margarine, Worcestershire sauce, celery salt, and garlic salt. Pour margarine mixture over cereal mixture. Toss until evenly coated. Spread in jelly roll pan. Bake in preheated 250° oven for 60 minutes. Stir every 15 minutes. Cool and store in a covered container.

Lavonne Ramaekers, Nebraska

PEOPLE CHOW
(For human consumption only!)

1 large box *Crispix* breakfast cereal
1 (11 oz.) pkg. milk chocolate
  chocolate chips

½ c. smooth peanut butter
Powdered sugar

Melt chocolate chips in microwave for 1 minute. Stir. Continue melting until melted. Do not microwave for longer than 1 minute at a time as the chocolate will burn. When chips are melted, add peanut butter. Return to microwave for 1 minute more. Stir well when done. Pour this mixture over cereal, stirring until all cereal is well coated with chocolate/peanut butter mixture. Put this mixture in a plastic garbage bag or a doubled grocery paper sack. Sprinkle 2 cups of powdered sugar over mixture, close bag, and shake well until all pieces are covered. You may need more powdered sugar according to taste. Store in an airtight container.

Daunita Cordes, Missouri

LITTLE SMOKIES

1 pkg. Little Smokies
1 lb. bacon

¾ lb. brown sugar
1 Tbsp. vinegar

Cut bacon strips in halves and wrap a half strip of bacon around each Little Smokie. Put seam side down in glass pan. Put the ¾ pound brown sugar to cover Little Smokies. Drizzle vinegar over the brown sugar and set in refrigerator overnight. Bake at 350° for 1 hour.

Donna Brua, Minnesota

SHRIMP PATE

A delectable spread I created for my food processor classes.

⅓ c. mayonnaise
1 (3 oz.) pkg. cream cheese, cut in
  cubes
3 Tbsp. chopped onion
¾ lb. cooked small shrimp, well-
  drained
1 Tbsp. white horseradish

1 tsp. Dijon-style mustard
1 tsp. dry dill
½ tsp. sugar
½ tsp. salt
1 Tbsp. lemon juice
¼ tsp. Tabasco sauce
Crackers or bread rounds

In a food processor fitted with the metal blade, combine mayonnaise and cream cheese. Add remaining ingredients and mix until blended. Shape into a ball or spoon into a crock. Refrigerate several hours or overnight for flavors to blend. May be refrigerated up to 2 days. Do not freeze. Serve pate with crackers or bread rounds. Makes 2 cups.

Rhonda Stevenson, AgriTalk

PERCOLATOR PUNCH
(Serves 20)

Put into percolator type coffee maker:

4 c. pineapple juice

6 c. apple cider

Put in basket:

3 sticks cinnamon   **2 tsp. whole cloves**

Percolate once. Serve hot.

Ken and Gail Root, AgriTalk

COCOA MIX

1 large box Nestle Quik   **³/₄ c. powdered sugar**
12 or 14 qt. size powdered milk   **1 small jar powdered cream**

Mix well and store in a covered container. Use about ⅓ cup dry mix to boiling water.

Debi Hensley, Kansas

FIRESIDE COFFEE MIX

2 c. non-dairy creamer   **2 c. sugar**
1½ c. hot cocoa mix   **2 tsp. cinnamon**
1½ c. instant coffee   **⅓ c. cocoa**

Mix well and store in a covered container. For 1 cup, use 1 cup boiling water to 2 to 4 tablespoons of the mix. Stir and add 1 heaping tablespoon whipped cream or ice cream and 1 cinnamon stick.

Shari Hoy, Florida

AMARETTO COFFEE CREAMER

³/₄ c. non-dairy creamer   **1 tsp. cinnamon**
³/₄ c. powdered sugar   **1 tsp. almond extract**

Combine in a jar or Tupperware. Put lid on and shake well. Add 2 tablespoons to a cup of coffee.

Debi Hensley, Kansas

HOT CRANBERRY TEA

1¼ c. sugar   **³/₄ c. lemon juice**
2 c. orange juice   **12 cloves**
1 qt. apple juice   **3 cinnamon sticks**
1 qt. cranberry juice   **1 qt. tea (2 tea bags)**

Combine, heat, and serve.

Shari Hoy, Florida

FROZEN SLUSH

Bananas   **Tropical Punch Kool-Aid**
Tang   **Ice**

In a blender, mix 1 or 2 bananas, 1 scoop of Tang, and 1 scoop of Tropical Punch Kool-Aid (both in powder form). Fill blender with ice. Add water and blend.

Don Evans, California

ICED TEA PUNCH

1 qt. water
2 fresh mint sprigs (good without, too)
8 small tea bags

1 c. sugar
6 oz. frozen limeade, thawed
6 oz. frozen lemonade, thawed

Bring 1 quart water to a boil and then add mint and tea bags. Cover and steep for 30 minutes. In gallon jar, mix sugar, limeade, and lemonade. Pour into hot tea mixture and add water to fill. Serve in tall glass over ice. Makes 20 (12 ounce) servings.

Roxanne Tubb, Texas

ORANGE DRINK

1 qt. reconstituted orange juice
1 pkg. noninstant vanilla pudding and pie filling

1 env. Dream Whip

In blender, pour orange juice and 1 package noninstant vanilla pudding and pie filling and blend a "second." Add 1 envelope Dream Whip. Blend a "second." *That's it.*

Lottie Evans, Texas

JELLO PUNCH

1 pkg. strawberry Jell-O
1 tall can pineapple juice
1 c. sugar

1 tall can frozen orange juice
1 pt. ginger ale (16 oz.)

Mix Jell-O in hot water as directed and add sugar while hot. Combine with orange juice (mixed with water according to directions) and pineapple juice. Add ginger ale after pouring in punch bowl (just before serving).

Punch, except for ginger ale, may be made several days in advance.

Pauline Hopper, Illinois

8

Soups, Salads

A HANDY SPICE AND HERB GUIDE

ALLSPICE—a pea-sized fruit that grows in Mexico, Jamaica, Central and South America. Its delicate flavor resembles a blend of cloves, cinnamon and nutmeg. USES: (Whole) Pickles, meats, boiled fish, gravies. (Ground) Puddings, relishes, fruit preserves, baking.

BASIL—the dried leaves and stems of an herb grown in the United States and North Mediterranean area. Has an aromatic, leafy flavor. USES: For flavoring tomato dishes and tomato paste, turtle soup; also use in cooked peas, squash, snap beans; sprinkle chopped over lamb chops and poultry.

BAY LEAVES—the dried leaves of an evergreen grown in the eastern Mediterranean countries. Has a sweet, herbaceous floral spice note. USES: For pickling, stews, for spicing sauces and soup. Also use with a variety of meats and fish.

CARAWAY—the seed of a plant grown in the Netherlands. Flavor that combines the tastes of Anise and Dill. USES: For the cordial Kummel, baking breads; often added to sauerkraut, noodles, cheese spreads. Also adds zest to French fried potatoes, liver, canned asparagus.

CURRY POWDER—a ground blend of ginger, turmeric, fenugreek seed, as many as 16 to 20 spices. USES: For all Indian curry recipes such as lamb, chicken, and rice, eggs, vegetables, and curry puffs.

DILL—the small, dark seed of the dill plant grown in India, having a clean, aromatic taste. USES: Dill is a predominant seasoning in pickling recipes; also adds pleasing flavor to sauerkraut, potato salad, cooked macaroni, and green apple pie.

MACE—the dried covering around the nutmeg seed. Its flavor is similar to nutmeg, but with a fragrant, delicate difference. USES: (Whole) For pickling, fish, fish sauce, stewed fruit. (Ground) Delicious in baked goods, pastries and doughnuts, adds unusual flavor to chocolate desserts.

MARJORAM—an herb of the mint family, grown in France and Chile. Has a minty-sweet flavor. USES: In beverages, jellies and to flavor soups, stews, fish, sauces. Also excellent to sprinkle on lamb while roasting.

MSG (MONOSODIUM GLUTAMATE)—is a vegetable protein derivative for raising the effectiveness of natural food flavors. USES: Small amounts, adjusted to individual taste, can be added to steaks, roasts, chops, seafoods, stews, soups, chowder, chop suey and cooked vegetables.

OREGANO—a plant of the mint family and a species of marjoram of which the dried leaves are used to make an herb seasoning. USES: An excellent flavoring for any tomato dish, especially pizza, chili con carne, and Italian specialties.

PAPRIKA—a mild, sweet red pepper growing in Spain, Central Europe and the United States. Slightly aromatic and prized for brilliant red color. USES: A colorful garnish for pale foods, and for seasoning Chicken Paprika, Hungarian Goulash, salad dressings.

POPPY—the seed of a flower grown in Holland. Has a rich fragrance and crunchy, nut-like flavor. USES: Excellent as a topping for breads, rolls and cookies. Also delicious in buttered noodles.

ROSEMARY—an herb (like a curved pine needle) grown in France, Spain, and Portugal, and having a sweet, fresh taste. USES: In lamb dishes, in soups, stews and to sprinkle on beef before roasting.

SAGE—the leaf of a shrub grown in Greece, Yugoslavia and Albania. Flavor is camphoraceous and minty. USES: For meat and poultry stuffing, sausages, meat loaf, hamburgers, stews and salads.

THYME—the leaves and stems of a shrub grown in France and Spain. Has a strong, distinctive flavor. USES: For poultry seasoning, in croquettes, fricassees and fish dishes. Also tasty on fresh sliced tomatoes.

TURMERIC—a root of the ginger family, grown in India, Haiti, Jamaica and Peru, having a mild, ginger-pepper flavor. USES: As a flavoring and coloring in prepared mustard and in combination with mustard as a flavoring for meats, dressings, salads.

SOUPS, SALADS

TACO SOUP

1 lb. hamburger
½ c. onion
2 (8 oz.) tomato sauce
2 cans undrained, stewed tomatoes

3 c. water
2 small cans chili beans
1 pkg. taco seasoning

Brown hamburger and onion. Mix in taco seasoning. Add the rest of the ingredients. Simmer ½ hour.

When serving: Break up Nacho cheese chips in bottom of bowl. Pour in some soup. Top with sour cream and shredded cheese.

Robin Miedema, North Dakota

POTATO SOUP

½ c. chopped celery
½ c. onion, diced
¼ c. margarine
2 c. diced ham
4 c. cubed potatoes

1 c. shredded carrots
1 c. corn
Salt and pepper to taste
4 to 6 c. water

Saute celery and onion in margarine. Mix all the rest of ingredients in large kettle. Cook and simmer with lid on 30 minutes. You may thicken before serving.

Iva Ungs, Iowa

OKRA GUMBO

2 c. sliced okra
2 c. diced tomatoes

1 c. chopped onions
¼ c. sugar

Combine all ingredients in heavy saucepan or Dutch oven. Barely cover with water. After mixture comes to a boil, reduce heat, cover pan with lid, and simmer over very low heat for 1 hour. Stir occasionally. Serve over rice or with fresh black-eyed peas.

Shirley Perrin, Texas

K.U. VEGETABLE SOUP

1 lb. beef stew meat
2 c. water
1 Tbsp. dehydrated onion
3 stalks celery, diced
2 Tbsp. uncooked rice
⅛ tsp. garlic powder
4 beef bouillon cubes

1 (16 oz.) can tomatoes
1 (10 oz.) can beef consomme
1 (6 oz.) can tomato juice
1 (16 oz.) bag frozen mixed
  vegetables
1 to 3 potatoes, peeled and cut into
  chunks

Brown meat. Add all ingredients, except frozen vegetables, and simmer for several hours until meat is tender. I don't add potatoes until I add the rest of the vegetables. Add more water, if necessary, and cook until vegetables are tender. I never make just one recipe.

Marie Etzenhouser, Kansas

BAKED POTATO SOUP

4 large baking potatoes
²/₃ c. butter or margarine
²/₃ c. all-purpose flour
6 c. milk
³/₄ tsp. salt
¹/₂ tsp. pepper
4 green onions, chopped and
    divided

12 slices bacon, cooked, crumbled,
    and divided
1¹/₄ c. (5 oz.) shredded Cheddar
    cheese, divided
1 (8 oz.) ctn. sour cream

Wash potatoes and prick several times with a fork. Bake at 400° for 1 hour or until done. Let cool. Cut potatoes in halves lengthwise, then scoop out the pulp.

Melt butter in a heavy saucepan over low heat; add the flour, stirring until smooth. Cook 1 minute, stirring constantly. Gradually add the 6 cups of milk; cook over medium heat, stirring constantly, until mixture is bubbly and has thickened.

Add potato pulp, salt, pepper, 2 tablespoons green onions, ¹/₂ cup bacon, and 1 cup cheese. Cook until thoroughly heated; stir in sour cream. Add extra milk, if necessary, for desired thickness. Serve with remaining onion, bacon, and cheese. Yields 10 cups.

Marie Etzenhouser, Kansas

SPICY BEEF BARLEY BEAN SOUP

Preparation time: 20 minutes. Cooking time: 25 minutes.

1 lb. ground beef (90% lean)
2 Tbsp. instant minced onion
1 Tbsp. olive oil
5 c. ready-to-serve beef broth
2 c. prepared chunky salsa (medium
    or hot)
1 c. julienned carrots (2 x ¹/₄ inch)

²/₃ c. quick barley
1 Tbsp. minced fresh basil
¹/₂ c. cauliflowerets
¹/₂ c. fresh *or* frozen peas
1 (15 *or* 16 oz.) red beans, rinsed
    and drained*
Basil sprigs

Brown ground beef with onion in oil in deep 12 inch skillet or Dutch oven, breaking into ³/₄ inch pieces, until beef is no longer pink. Pour off drippings if necessary. Add beef broth, salsa, carrots, barley, and minced basil. Bring to a boil; reduce heat to medium. Cook, uncovered, 10 minutes, stirring occasionally. Add cauliflowerets and peas; continue cooking until vegetables are crisp-tender, about 6 minutes. Add beans; heat through. Ladle into soup tureen; garnish with basil sprigs. Makes 4 servings.

Note: If thinner soup is desired, additional beef broth may be added.

* One 15 *or* 16 ounce can kidney beans or shelled beans may be substituted.

Recipe reprinted by permission from the National Beef Cook-Off sponsored by the American National CattleWomen and in cooperation with the Beef Industry Council.

Ann Holz, Temple, New Hampshire

NEBRASKA SLAW
(Salad)

1 medium head cauliflower,
   chopped
1 medium head cabbage, shredded

1 medium onion, chopped fine
1 lb. bacon, fried crisp and
   crumbled

Dressing:

2 c. Miracle Whip
3 Tbsp. sugar
1/4 tsp. pepper

1 Tbsp. vinegar
1/2 tsp. salt
1/3 to 1/2 c. Parmesan cheese

Layer alternately the vegetables and dressing. Cover and chill several hours or overnight. Toss just before serving. This makes a quite large salad.

Shirley Hoffman, Nebraska

TAFFY APPLE SALAD

1 large can pineapple chunks (drain
   off juice)
1 1/2 Tbsp. vinegar

1/3 c. sugar
1 egg
1 Tbsp. flour

Mix and boil until it thickens; cool.

Mix in:

8 oz. Cool Whip
2 chopped apples with skin

1 1/2 c. peanuts
2 c. mini marshmallows

Caryl Rieckman, Oklahoma

HOT CHICKEN SALAD

2 c. cooked chicken, cut up (white
   meat preferred)
1 c. cooked rice
1 can chicken soup (undiluted)
1 Tbsp. fresh minced onion
1 c. celery, cut in small pieces

1 Tbsp. lemon juice
1 tsp. salt
3/4 c. mayonnaise
1/2 c. sliced water chestnuts, cut fine
1 c. corn flakes, crushed
1/2 c. almonds, chopped fine

Saute celery a few minutes. Mix all ingredients, but corn flakes and almonds. Put in greased 9x13 inch casserole dish. Sprinkle almonds and corn flakes over top and bake at 350° for about 30 minutes.

I have made this many times for church, funeral, lunches and have been asked for recipe many, many times. For funeral lunches, I do not add corn flakes nor almonds. *It is good.*

Marjorie Cox, Iowa

CIRCUS PEANUT SALAD

14 pieces circus peanut candy
2 pkg. (3 oz.) orange gelatin
2 c. hot water
1 medium can crushed pineapple,
   drained (save juice)

2 c. celery, chopped fine
1/2 c. chopped nuts
1 small ctn. whipped topping

Melt and dissolve circus peanut candies in hot water. Add gelatin. Measure pineapple juice, adding cold water to make 2 cups. Add to gelatin mixture. Chill until partially set. Add pineapple, celery, and nuts, stirring well. Fold in whipped topping. Put in 9x13 inch pan and refrigerate.

Carolyn Hoffer, Minnesota

TROPICAL SALAD

1 can white cherries, pitted
1 (12 oz.) pkg. cocoanut
1 pkg. mini marshmallows

1 medium can crushed pineapple
½ c. maraschino cherries
½ c. walnuts, broken (big pieces)

Mix together. Add 1 carton sour cream. Chill overnight.

Bunny Adams, Kansas

FOUR BEAN SALAD

1 c. cooked or canned, drained
   green beans
1 c. drained wax beans
1 c. drained kidney beans

1 c. cooked soybeans
½ c. diced celery
½ c. sliced onion

Mix together:

¼ c. soy oil
¼ to ½ c. sugar

¼ c. vinegar

Boil. Pour over bean mixture. Refrigerate 24 hours before serving. Makes 12 servings.

Nutritional value (per serving): 101 calories, 0 mg cholesterol, 3 g protein, 142 mg sodium, and 6 g fat.

Reprinted with permission from the Minnesota Soybean Research and Promotion Council.

GREEN SOYBEAN SALAD

2 c. cooked green soybeans,
   drained
1 c. diced celery
1 Tbsp. chopped parsley

1 c. raw cauliflower flowerets
1 Tbsp. chives or green onions
¼ tsp. basil

Toss everything together with salad greens and serve with mayonnaise or your favorite dressing. Soybeans should be cooked before removing them from the pod. Serves 6.

Nutritional value (per serving): 103 calories, 0 mg cholesterol, 10 g protein, 11 mg sodium, 5 g fat, 7 g carbohydrates, and 67 mg calcium.

Reprinted with permission from the Minnesota Soybean Research and Promotion Council.

STRAWBERRY-ROMAINE SALAD

1 c. vegetable oil
¾ c. sugar
½ c. red wine vinegar
2 cloves garlic, minced
½ tsp. salt
½ tsp. paprika
¼ tsp. ground white pepper

1 large head romaine lettuce
1 head Boston lettuce
1 pt. strawberries, sliced
1 c. (4 oz.) shredded Monterey Jack
    cheese
½ c. chopped walnuts, toasted

Combine first 7 ingredients in a large jar. Cover tightly and shake vigorously. May be refrigerated up to 1 week.

Tear lettuce into bite-size pieces. Combine torn lettuce, strawberries, cheese, and walnuts in a large salad bowl. Shake dressing vigorously. Pour over salad and toss gently. Serves 12 people.

To give more color, add a little fresh spinach.

Marie Etzenhouser, Kansas

HEAVENLY CHEESE SALAD

Dissolve one 3 ounce package lemon jello in 1 cup boiling water. Add ¾ cup pineapple juice. Chill until slightly thickened.

Fold:

1 c. shredded cheese (Longhorn or
    Cheddar)
1 can crushed pineapple (1 to 1¾
    c.)

1 c. cream, whipped, or Cool Whip

Pour into a 1½ quart mold. Let set several hours. When ready to serve, unmold on lettuce leaves. Garnish as desired.

Ritz crackers may be served with this.

Bertha Traver, Iowa

BLUEBERRY SALAD

1 (6 oz.) box raspberry jello
1 can blueberry pie filling

1 (20 oz.) can crushed pineapple,
    drained (save juice)

Dissolve jello in 2 cups boiling water. The reserved pineapple juice works well in this. Mix the pie filling, pineapple, and jello together. Put into a bowl and refrigerate.

Topping:

8 oz. cream cheese
8 oz. sour cream

½ c. sugar

Mix together. Spread over jello. Can sprinkle nuts on top.

When I make this, I use a tall sided clear bowl to see this attractive salad. It is very delicious.

Mary Ann Thompson, Kansas

CASHEW SALAD

4½ c. mixture of 3 kinds of lettuce (such as red leaf, romaine, and Boston), washed and torn into bite-size pieces

½ head cauliflower, broken into bite-size pieces
¾ c. cashews

For dressing:

1 small red onion, coarsely chopped
¼ c. vinegar
¾ c. sugar
⅛ tsp. ground black pepper

1 tsp. celery seed
2 tsp. prepared mustard
1 c. olive oil

Toss together lettuce, cauliflower, and cashews. Place onion and vinegar in blender and blend until onions are finely chopped. Add sugar, pepper, celery seed, mustard, and oil. Blend. When ready to serve, toss with dressing to taste or serve dressing on side. Makes about 6 servings.

APRICOT MOLD

1 (3 oz.) 4 serving size pkg. apricot Jell-O
4½ Tbsp. sugar
1 flat can crushed pineapple with juice

1½ c. buttermilk
4 oz. whipped topping

Combine dry Jell-O, sugar, and pineapple in saucepan. Stir. Bring to a boil. Remove from heat and cool. Add buttermilk and fold in topping. Pour into mold and chill in refrigerator until congealed.

Velma Hitchcock, Texas

PINK CLOUD SALAD

1 can Eagle Brand sweetened condensed milk
1 Tbsp. lemon juice
1 can cherry pie filling

1 flat can crushed pineapple, drained
1 large (12 oz.) ctn. Cool Whip

Mix all ingredients together in large mixing bowl. Since this is a large amount, it may be divided and half frozen for later use. Chill in refrigerator until congealed.

Ida Jones, Texas

CABBAGE SALAD FOR FREEZER

2 medium size heads cabbage
2 large carrots, shredded

1 green and 1 red pepper (optional)

Dressing:

3 c. sugar
2 c. vinegar
1 c. water

1 tsp. mustard seeds
1 tsp. celery seeds

Mix and boil 5 minutes. Add seeds. May be made ahead of time.

Chop cabbage and sprinkle with 1 teaspoon salt. Let stand 1 hour. Drain off liquid well. Add shredded carrots and peppers. Pour chilled syrup over vegetables.

May be frozen - thawed and serve.

Bertha Traver, Iowa

CRANBERRY FLUFF

2 c. ground cranberries
3 c. miniature marshmallows
1 c. sugar
2 c. diced apples
1 small can crushed pineapple,
    drained

½ c. nuts (optional)
1 pkg. dessert topping mix,
    whipped (or Cool Whip)
¼ tsp. salt

Combine cranberries, marshmallows, and sugar; refrigerate for 12 hours. Combine remaining ingredients; add to cranberry mixture. Refrigerate for several hours. Yield: 10 to 12 servings.

This makes a beautiful complement to your holiday festivities served in a compote ... and it is delicious!

Jan Bell, Iowa

TAPIOCA SALAD

5 c. water   1 c. small pearl tapioca

Boil 30 minutes on low to simmer. Stir often.

Add:

1 box strawberry jello   1 c. cold water
1 c. sugar

Refrigerate overnight. The next morning, stir to loosen everything.

Add:

10 oz. Cool Whip
1 box frozen strawberries (juice and
    all)

Stir till blended. Can add chopped bananas if you like. Refrigerate.

Mrs. Dorothy Pfingsten, Illinois

STICKY RICE SALAD

1 c. white rice   2 c. water

Simmer until warm is absorbed.

Add:

3 c. milk   1 c. sugar

Cook until milk is absorbed. Stir several times - it scorches easily. Cool well, then add 2 cups whipped cream. Keeps very well in fridge.

Eva Messer, North Dakota

CARROT SALAD

1 (3 oz.) pkg. orange gelatin
1 (8 oz.) pkg. cream cheese,
  softened
1½ c. miniature marshmallows
1 c. boiling water

1 (8 oz.) can crushed pineapple
  (including juice)
1 c. grated carrots
1 env. Dream Whip

Stir first 4 ingredients together until dissolved. Add pineapple and carrots. Prepare Dream Whip according to package direction, omitting vanilla, and add to mixture, mixing well. Put mixture into large mold and for individual servings, fill cupcake cups with ⅓ cup of mixture. When making individual servings, place filled cups in cupcake tins to mold.

Pauline Hopper, Illinois

BLUEBERRY SALAD

2 (3 oz.) pkg. red raspberry gelatin
2 c. boiling water
1 can blueberry pie filling

1 env. Dream Whip, prepared
6 oz. softened cream cheese

Dissolve 1 package of gelatin in 1 cup boiling water. Let cool slightly. Add can of blueberry pie filling to cooled gelatin; mix well. Pour into a 9 inch square pan. Refrigerate until set.

Dissolve other package of gelatin in 1 cup boiling water. Refrigerate until slightly set.

Prepare Dream Whip as directed on package; blend in softened cream cheese. Add this to plain gelatin and whip with beater until blended. Spread on top of blueberry mixture. Refrigerate at least 1 hour. Cut into squares and serve.

Aldene Winquist, Iowa

HOT GERMAN POTATO SALAD

6 boiled eggs
5 lb. potatoes
3 medium size onions
1 c. celery, cut fine
2 tsp. salt
Little pepper

1 lb. bacon, cut into small pieces
2 Tbsp. flour
½ c. vinegar
½ c. warm water
1 c. sugar

Cook potatoes; peel and slice. Add onion, celery, and chopped eggs. Keep warm. Fry bacon crisp, then drain. Leave ½ of the warm bacon grease in the skillet. Stir in flour and sugar. Add vinegar, water, salt, and pepper. Cook well, then pour over potatoes. Mix gently.

Marlene Fudge, Indiana

16

PRETZEL SALAD

1 (6 oz.) pkg. jello (strawberry)
1½ to 2 c. hot water
2 (10 oz.) pkg. frozen strawberries
3 Tbsp. granulated sugar
2 c. crushed pretzels (put in Baggie
    and roll with rolling pin)

¾ c. melted butter or margarine
8 oz. cream cheese, softened
½ c. sugar
8 oz. container Cool Whip

Dissolve jello in hot water. (If strawberry has a lot of juice, only use 1½ cups water.) Stir in strawberries. Put in refrigerator to thicken.

Mix 3 tablespoons sugar, 2 cups pretzels, and ¾ cup melted margarine. Press mixture firmly in 9x13 inch greased baking pan until flat. Bake 15 minutes at 350°. Put aside to cool.

Cream together cream cheese and ½ cup sugar. Fold in Cool Whip. Spread over crust when cool. Put jello and strawberries over the top. Chill.

Caryl Rieckman, Oklahoma

CANDY APPLE SALAD

1 c. dairy sour cream
8 oz. Cool Whip
4 c. diced apples
2 c. miniature marshmallows

1 c. dates, chopped
3 large Snickers candy bars, cut
    into small pieces

Mix sour cream and Cool Whip in a large bowl. Add apples, marshmallows, dates, and candy pieces. Stir well. Put into covered bowl and refrigerate overnight.

Iva Ungs, Iowa

CORN BREAD SALAD

1 (10 inch) pan corn bread, cooked
    and crumbled up
1 small onion
½ c. mayonnaise

2 tomatoes
1 green bell pepper
1 tsp. mustard

Cook 1 pan corn bread. Crumble. Add 1 small chopped onion, 2 chopped tomatoes, 1 chopped green bell pepper, ½ cup mayonnaise, and 1 teaspoon mustard. Mix and serve.

Ethel Montgomery, Texas

FROZEN BUTTERMILK SALAD

1½ c. buttermilk
1 c. sugar
1 can crushed pineapple with juice

3 mashed bananas
8 oz. Cool Whip

Mix buttermilk and sugar together. Add other ingredients and freeze in a 9x13 inch pan.

Susan D. Swift, Missouri

SURPRISE SALAD

1 pkg. spinach, washed and cut or torn in pieces

Dressing:

2 Tbsp. sesame seeds
¼ tsp. paprika
¼ c. sugar
¼ c. vinegar

1 pt. fresh strawberries, sliced

⅓ c. oil
4 Tbsp. Worcestershire sauce
1 Tbsp. minced or sliced red onion

Mix dressing and pour over spinach and strawberries. Toss lightly.

Note: An easy, good salad - even if spinach isn't high on your choice of greens.

Rosalie Nelsen, Nebraska

CRANBERRY SALAD

1 bag raw cranberries, washed and sorted (run through food grinder or processor)
1 orange (rind and all)
1 (3 oz.) box orange jello (may use raspberry)
1 c.. chopped celery

1 c. chopped marshmallows
1 c. chopped nuts
1 c. crushed drained pineapple
1 c. granulated sugar
Pinch of salt
½ c. cold water (optional)

Let set and serve.

We like orange jello best - we have also added 2 chopped apples, skin and all.

Nancy Matlock, Indiana

SPINACH SALAD

Bring to a boil:

½ c. sugar

¼ c. vinegar

Let cool. Add ½ cup vegetable oil. Refrigerate. Keeps for weeks.

When ready to use, add spinach, salt, pepper, and paprika to taste. At the last, add toasted sesame seeds.

Can add 4 ounces sliced thin mushrooms, hard-boiled egg, sliced green onions, and real bacon bits.

Nellie Value, Iowa

PHILADELPHIA CREAM CHEESE SALAD

2 small pkg. lemon gelatin
1 (No. 303) can crushed drained pineapple
1 (10 oz.) jar maraschino cherries, cut in pieces

1 c. pecans, chopped
1 (8 oz.) pkg. Philadelphia cream cheese, softened
½ c. whipping cream

Make gelatin and let partially set. Beat whipping cream until fluffy. Add cream cheese and continue beating, a small amount at a time, then add gelatin. Mix until well blended. Add pineapple, cherries, and pecans. Mix well. Pour into 13x13 inch dish or large bowl. Let set overnight.

Edna Michaelis, Illinois

CAULIFLOWER SALAD

1 small head cauliflower, chopped in
    bite-size
1/3 c. fine chopped onion
1/3 c. sliced radishes

1/2 c. chopped green olives
2 c. chopped broccoli
1 c. grated medium Cheddar cheese

Dressing - Mix together:

1 c. Hellmann's mayonnaise
1 c. sour cream

1 pkg. Hidden Valley Ranch dressing
    mix

Pour over vegetable mixture and stir well. Chill several hours and serve.

Sherri Clauson, Iowa

CHARTREUSE SALAD

1 1/2 c. crushed pineapple
1/2 pt. coffee cream
2 pkg. lime Jell-O
2 c. water (hot)

1 (3 oz.) pkg. cream cheese
1 c. chopped pecans
1 1/2 c. chopped celery

Drain pineapple well. Heat water and dissolve Jell-O in water. Add pineapple juice. Chill.

Marsha L. Thomas, Indiana

PEAS AND CORN SALAD

1 can drained peas
1 can drained corn
1 large green pepper, diced

1 large red onion, diced
1 c. celery, chopped

Cook to dissolve:

1/4 c. oil
1/2 c. vinegar

1 tsp. salt
3/4 c. sugar

Mix together. Refrigerate. Keeps a long time.

Lois Ruff, Iowa

Notes

Vegetables

EQUIVALENT CHART

3 tsp.	1 Tbsp.	¼ lb. crumbled Bleu cheese	1 c.
2 Tbsp.	⅛ c.	1 lemon	3 Tbsp. juice
4 Tbsp.	¼ c.	1 orange	⅓ c. juice
8 Tbsp.	½ c.	1 lb. unshelled walnuts	1½ to 1¾ c. shelled
16 Tbsp.	1 c.	2 c. fat	1 lb.
5 Tbsp. + 1 tsp.	⅓ c.	1 lb. butter	2 c. or 4 sticks
12 Tbsp.	¾ c.	2 c. granulated sugar	1 lb.
4 oz.	½ c.	3½-4 c. unsifted powdered sugar	1 lb.
8 oz.	1 c.	2¼ c. packed brown sugar	1 lb.
16 oz.	1 lb.	4 c. sifted flour	1 lb.
1 oz.	2 Tbsp. fat or liquid	4½ c. cake flour	1 lb.
2 c.	1 pt.	3½ c. unsifted whole wheat flour	1 lb.
2 pt.	1 qt.	4 oz. (1 to 1¼ c.) uncooked	
1 qt.	4 c.	macaroni	2¼ c. cooked
⅝ c.	½ c. + 2 Tbsp.	7 oz. spaghetti	4 c. cooked
⅞ c.	¾ c. + 2 Tbsp.	4 oz. (1½ to 2 c.) uncooked	
1 jigger	1½ fl. oz. (3 Tbsp.)	noodles	2 c. cooked
8 to 10 egg whites	1 c.	28 saltine crackers	1 c. crumbs
12 to 14 egg yolks	1 c.	4 slices bread	1 c. crumbs
1 c. unwhipped cream	2 c. whipped	14 square graham crackers	1 c. crumbs
1 lb. shredded American cheese	4 c.	22 vanilla wafers	1 c. crumbs

SUBSTITUTIONS FOR A MISSING INGREDIENT

1 square **chocolate** (1 ounce) = 3 or 4 tablespoons cocoa plus ½ tablespoon fat

1 tablespoon **cornstarch** (for thickening) = 2 tablespoons flour

1 cup sifted **all-purpose flour** = 1 cup plus 2 tablespoons sifted cake flour

1 cup sifted **cake flour** = 1 cup minus 2 tablespoons sifted all-purpose flour

1 teaspoon **baking powder** = ¼ teaspoon baking soda plus ½ teaspoon cream of tartar

1 cup **sour milk** = 1 cup sweet milk into which 1 tablespoon vinegar or lemon juice has been stirred

1 cup **sweet milk** = 1 cup sour milk or buttermilk plus ½ teaspoon baking soda

¾ cup **cracker crumbs** = 1 cup bread crumbs

1 cup **cream, sour, heavy** = ⅓ cup butter and ⅔ cup milk in any sour milk recipe

1 teaspoon **dried herbs** = 1 tablespoon fresh herbs

1 cup **whole milk** = ½ cup evaporated milk and ½ cup water or 1 cup reconstituted nonfat dry milk and 1 tablespoon butter

2 ounces **compressed yeast** = 3 (¼ ounce) packets of dry yeast

1 tablespoon **instant minced onion, rehydrated** = 1 small fresh onion

1 tablespoon **prepared mustard** = 1 teaspoon dry mustard

⅛ teaspoon **garlic powder** = 1 small pressed clove of garlic

1 lb. **whole dates** = 1½ cups, pitted and cut

3 medium **bananas** = 1 cup mashed

3 cups **dry corn flakes** = 1 cup crushed

10 **miniature marshmallows** = 1 large marshmallow

GENERAL OVEN CHART

Very slow oven	250° to 300°F.
Slow oven	300° to 325°F.
Moderate oven	325° to 375°F.
Medium hot oven	375° to 400°F.
Hot oven	400° to 450°F.
Very hot oven	450° to 500°F.

CONTENTS OF CANS

Of the different sizes of cans used by commercial canners, the most common are:

Size:	Average Contents
8 oz.	1 cup
Picnic	1¼ cups
No. 300	1¾ cups
No. 1 tall	2 cups
No. 303	2 cups
No. 2	2½ cups
No. 2½	3½ cups
No. 3	4 cups
No. 10	12 to 13 cups

VEGETABLES

MY OWN BAKED BEANS

The following is a recipe, one that I created myself to serve our large family years ago.

4 c. Great Northern beans (2 lb.)
1/2 to 1 lb. Ranch Style bacon, cut
   into small pieces
2 large onions, cut up
1 Tbsp. salt
1/4 tsp. pepper

2 Tbsp. Grandma's molasses
2 Tbsp. prepared mustard
1/2 c. white sugar
1/2 c. brown sugar
2 c. catsup

Soak the beans overnight. Next morning, cover with clean water after draining (10 quart pan). Simmer slowly about 1 hour. While simmering, saute bacon long enough to fry out half the fat, then add to beans along with rest of ingredients. Put into 350° oven and bake for 4 to 6 hours, covered. Bake until tender and brown, stirring occasionally. Add water if they become too dry while baking.

Evelyn Miller, Iowa

CREAMY BROCCOLI CASSEROLE

2 eggs
1 (10 3/4 oz.) can condensed cream of
   mushroom soup (undiluted)
1 c. mayonnaise
3/4 c. chopped nuts
1 medium onion, chopped

2 (10 oz.) pkg. frozen chopped
   broccoli, cooked and drained
1 c. (4 oz.) shredded Cheddar
   cheese
1 Tbsp. butter, melted
1/4 c. soft bread crumbs

In a bowl, beat eggs. Add soup, mayonnaise, nuts, and onions. Stir in broccoli; pour into greased 2 quart shallow baking dish. Sprinkle with cheese. Combine butter and bread crumbs; sprinkle on top. Bake, uncovered, at 350° for 30 minutes. Makes 8 to 10 servings.

This is really delicious! One of our favorites.

Lorraine Carle, New York

SCALLOPED CORN

1 (16 oz.) can cream style corn
1 (16 oz.) can whole kernel corn
1 c. sour cream
1/2 c. melted butter

2 eggs, beaten
1 box Jiffy corn bread mix (8 1/2 oz.
   box Jiffy corn muffin mix)
1 c. shredded cheese

Mix all together, but cheese. Put in greased 9x13 inch baking dish. Bake at 350° for 30 minutes. Add cheese over top and bake 10 minutes more. *Delicious.*

Marjorie Cox, Iowa

SWISS BAKED POTATOES

This is a recipe a dairy farmer shared with me when we lived in Green Bay, Wisconsin. I have never seen it anywhere else nor come across anyone who has made the dish before. It is a favorite of all our family and goes well with any meal. It really dresses up otherwise bland potatoes.

3 large baking potatoes, peeled
1/4 c. butter, melted
Salt, pepper

1 c. shredded Swiss cheese
2 to 3 Tbsp. grated Parmesan cheese

Halve potatoes lengthwise, then cut crosswise in 1/8 inch slices. Immediately put in glass pan with slices overlapping, arranged in serving portions. Pour butter over potatoes; season with salt and pepper. Bake for 20 minutes at 500°. Remove from oven and sprinkle with Swiss cheese, then with Parmesan cheese. Bake an additional 5 to 7 minutes or until cheese is melted and slightly browned. Serve immediately.

Note: Do not precut potatoes and set them aside or they will turn brown.

Rich and Sharon Hull, AgriTalk

CORN CASSEROLE

1 (16 oz.) can creamed corn
1 (5 oz.) can milk
1/2 lb. bacon
1 stick margarine

1 egg
1 c. chopped onion
1 c. chopped green bell peppers
1 c. crushed Ritz crackers

Microwave bacon until crisp. Set aside. Saute peppers and onions in a little bacon drippings. Add milk and beaten egg with corn, peppers, and onions. Mix crumbled bacon with corn mixture (all but 2 slices). Melt margarine and add enough of the crackers for a crust in a baking dish. Pour corn mixture into the dish and add remaining crackers for top crust along with the 2 slices of bacon. Bake 30 minutes at 300°.

Louise Evans, Texas

SCALLOPED CORN

2 slightly beaten eggs
1/2 c. milk
1 Tbsp. sugar
1 tsp. salt
Pepper

2 slices cubed bread
1/3 c. chopped onion
1 can cream corn
1 c. Rice Krispies, crushed
4 Tbsp. melted butter

Combine eggs, milk, sugar, salt, pepper, bread, onion, and corn and put in casserole. Mix butter and Rice Krispies and sprinkle over mixture. Bake 50 minutes at 350°.

Katherine Olson, Minnesota

SOUTHWEST HOMINY

This is the recipe that was given to me by the wife of a farm broadcaster in Wichita Falls, Texas. She passed away last year and was an excellent cook. This recipe turns ordinary bland hominy into a dish that goes well with anything but especially Mexican or Southwest foods.

1 medium size onion
1 stick butter
1 can drained yellow corn

1 can drained hominy
1 c. sour cream
Salt and pepper

Saute 1 chopped onion in the butter till tender. Add corn and hominy. Season to taste. Add 1 cup sour cream. Mix together over heat until bubbles. Put in glass container and bake for 30 minutes at 300°.

Rich and Sharon Hull, AgriTalk

CHEESE CORN

2 c. or more drained corn	2 Tbsp. sugar
(homegrown frozen is the best)	2 eggs
Salt and pepper	1/3 c. milk
2 Tbsp. margarine	1/2 lb. Velveeta cheese
2 Tbsp. flour	

Add 2 tablespoons margarine to drained corn and stir. Mix in 2 tablespoons flour. Mix in 2 tablespoons sugar. Add 2 beaten eggs and 1/3 cup milk; stir. Add Velveeta. Bake at 350° for 35 minutes.

Susan Wedemeyer, Iowa

GOLDEN CORN BAKE

1 onion, chopped	1 pkg. Jiffy corn muffin mix
1/2 green pepper, chopped	3 eggs, beaten
1 stick oleo	1/4 c. pimento
1 can whole kernel corn	1 c. sour cream (commercial)
1 can cream style corn	1 c. grated Cheddar cheese

Saute onion and pepper in oleo. Add corn, eggs, and muffin mix. Put in greased casserole. Top with sour cream and cheese. Bake in 350° oven for 45 to 60 minutes.

Ruth Kenaley, Iowa

NEBRASKA CORN CASSEROLE

1 can whole kernel corn, drained	1 c. Velveeta cheese
1 can cream style corn	1 c. shell macaroni (raw)
2 Tbsp. onion, chopped	3/4 c. milk
1 stick oleo	

Mix all together. Bake at 350° for 1 hour. *Very good.*

Shirley Hoffman, Nebraska

POTATO CASSEROLE

2 lb. hash browns (your own or	1/2 c. chopped onion
frozen ones, thawed)	1/2 c. milk
2 c. sour cream (dairy)	2 c. grated Cheddar cheese
1 can mushroom soup	Salt and pepper

Mix sour cream, mushroom soup, and milk; add onion. Stir in hash browns and cheese. Add seasonings. Bake in a 7x11 inch greased dish for 45 minutes to 1 hour at 350°.

Iva Ungs, Iowa

HASH BROWN POTATO CASSEROLE

2 lb. frozen hash brown potatoes
1/2 c. melted oleo or butter
2 tsp. salt
1/2 tsp. pepper
1 medium onion, chopped

1 can cream of chicken soup
1 pt. sour cream
10 oz. Cheddar cheese, grated
Crushed potato chips for topping

Mix all ingredients together. Pour into buttered Pyrex dish. Cover with crushed potato chips. Do not cover. Bake at 300° for 1 hour.

Shirley Perrin, Texas

HAWAIIAN YAMS

3 to 4 lb. yams
1 c. apricot nectar
1 c. pineapple juice

2 Tbsp. butter
1/2 c. sugar
1 can unsweetened pineapple slices

Peel yams and cut in 4 pieces each. Cover with cold water. Boil until nearly tender. Drain and cool. When cool, slice in 1/2 inch slices.

In large skillet, melt butter. Add sugar, apricot nectar, and juice from pineapple slices. Cook over medium heat until thickened. Add sliced yams to coat with syrup. Pour into casserole, arranging neatly. Bake in preheated 350° oven for 30 minutes. Cover with pineapple slices halfway through baking. Serves 6.

Such a nice alternative to yams with marshmallows.

Marilyn Denny, Minnesota

SCALLOPED POTATOES

6 c. potatoes, sliced
Salt
Pepper
1 can cream of chicken soup

1/4 c. water
1 c. Velveeta, cubed
1 small onion, chopped

Heat soup, water, and cheese until melted. Mix with potatoes and onion. Put in dish and bake at 375° for 1 hour. When center bubbles, reduce to 350° and bake until done.

Kristie Reierson, Iowa

OVEN BAKED BEANS

Boil 1 pound of navy beans until tender, but firm. Place in a casserole dish or Corning Ware.

Add to the beans:

1/2 c. catsup
1/2 c. molasses (dark kind)
1/2 c. brown sugar

Salt and pepper to taste
1/2 lb. smoked bacon or ham, cut in small pieces

Bake in a 350° oven for 2 hours.

These are good either served hot or cold.

Marie Beymer, Iowa

QUICK BAKED BEANS

1 Tbsp. oil	**12 oz. bacon, cut into pieces**
½ c. chopped onion	

Mix the preceding in saucepan and cook till bacon is browned. Drain grease.

Add:

2 cans pork and beans	**1 tsp. mustard**
¼ c. brown sugar	**1 tsp. Worcestershire sauce**

Dissolve 2 tablespoons cornstarch in a little water and add to bean mixture. Cook on medium heat till beans return to original color.

This tastes like it's been baking for hours.

Peg Fast, South Dakota

BARBEQUED GREEN BEANS

Fry or microwave 2 strips of bacon that have been diced.

Add:

Bacon plus 2 Tbsp. bacon fat	**½ c. sugar and 1 tsp. corn starch,**
1 large onion, lightly browned (or	**mixed together**
use dried onion flakes)	**¼ c. vinegar**
½ c. catsup	

Stir and simmer until thick. Add 2 cans (16 ounces) *drained* cut green beans or frozen cooked and/or fresh cooked green beans. Simmer until hot. Serve and enjoy.

Goes very well with "Mountain Oysters" or other beef dishes.

Grace Lupfer, Kansas

ZUCCHINI SKILLET

1 lb. ground beef	**1¼ c. whole kernel corn (about 3**
1 onion, chopped	**medium cobs)**
¼ c. green pepper, chopped	**2 Tbsp. pimentos, chopped**
1 clove garlic, minced	**¼ c. chopped parsley**
5 small zucchini or summer squash,	**1¼ tsp. salt**
sliced	**¼ tsp. pepper**
2 large tomatoes, peeled and	**1 to 2 Tbsp. chili powder**
chopped	

Saute beef, onions, and garlic until well browned. Add remaining ingredients. Cover and simmer 10 to 15 minutes or until vegetables are tender. Serves 6.

Mrs. Victor Euteneuer, Minnesota

BAKED SQUASH

Yellow crookneck squash	**Salt**
1 beaten egg	**Pepper**
¼ c. milk	**Ritz crackers**
2 Tbsp. margarine	**Grated cheese**
Onion to taste	

Cook squash in a saucepan in a very small amount of water until tender. Drain. Add 1 beaten egg, ¼ cup milk, 2 tablespoons margarine, onion to taste, salt, and pepper. Add crumbled Ritz crackers to thicken. Put in a buttered casserole dish. Cook at 350° until firm. Top with Ritz cracker crumbs and grated cheese.

Frances Stallings, Texas

BROCCOLI-RICE CASSEROLE

2 pkg. frozen whole broccoli,
    cooked as directed
1 c. (uncooked) rice, cooked
1 can cream of mushroom soup
1 can cream of chicken soup

1 medium onion, chopped
½ c. celery, chopped
1 small jar Cheez Whiz
2 Tbsp. oleo

Saute onion and celery in oleo until tender. Add soups. Heat. Butter a 7½ x 12 inch Pyrex dish. Layer the broccoli and rice and pour the mixture over all. Bake at 300° for approximately 25 minutes, or until bubbling.

E. Jones, Texas

DELICIOUS "SAUERKRAUT SUPREME"

1 (No. 2) can (1 qt.) kraut, drained
1 to 2 c. diced tomatoes
1 medium onion

4 slices bacon
1 c. brown sugar

Dice bacon and fry; add onions and saute. Add kraut. Mix brown sugar and tomatoes. Pour over kraut mixture. Simmer; pour in casserole. Bake 40 minutes at 350° or leave on stove for 1 hour, simmering.

Karen S. Taylor, Illinois

CABBAGE AND NOODLES CASSEROLE

4 slices bacon, diced
1 Tbsp. butter
1 large onion, sliced thin
2 cloves garlic, minced
1 c. chicken broth
½ tsp. salt

½ tsp. fresh black pepper
1½ lb. head cabbage, shredded
8 oz. medium no-yolk egg noodles,
    fresh cooked and drained
2 tsp. poppy seeds

In large electric wok, cook bacon until crisp. Remove to paper towel. Drain off and discard all but 1 teaspoon fat from wok. Add butter, onions, and garlic and cook until translucent. Add chicken broth, salt, and pepper. Bring to a boil and boil 1 minute. Add cabbage. Stir-fry until nearly done. Stir in drained bacon and then fold in noodles and poppy seeds. Cook just until noodles are hot. Serves 8.

This is so unusual and so good. Even people who don't care for cabbage gobble it up. Besides, it's low calorie.

Marilyn Denny, Minnesota

26

PARADISE VEGETABLE-PASTA SUPREME

2 lb. spiral pasta
2 cucumbers, cubed
1 small can chopped olives
  (optional)
3 to 4 tomatoes, chopped
1 small jar pimentos, chopped

1 onion, diced
1 (4 oz.) can green chilies, diced
1 jar Schilling Salad Supreme (I use
  ¼)
1 large bottle Wish-Bone Italian
  dressing

Cook and drain pasta. Toss with cucumbers, tomatoes, olives, pimento, onions, chilies, Salad Supreme, and dressing.

Recipe may be made in half. *Ideal for large group.*

Mrs. Donald Traver, Iowa

PICKLED VEGETABLES

1 (20 oz.) bag frozen cauliflower,
  broccoli, and carrots
1 c. vinegar
1 c. sugar
½ c. salad oil

1 c. chopped celery
½ c. chopped onion
½ c. chopped green peppers
Salt and pepper to taste

Cook frozen vegetables according to directions on bag. Boil vinegar, sugar, salt, and pepper for 5 minutes. Add celery, onion, and green peppers. Pour over cooked vegetables. Refrigerate. Keeps several weeks.

Mrs. Dorothy Pfingsten, Illinois

ASPARAGUS CASSEROLE

1 can mushroom soup
¼ lb. Velveeta cheese
1 tsp. margarine
1 (14 oz.) can asparagus, drained

2 to 3 medium boiled potatoes
2 hard cooked eggs
Pepper to taste
No salt

Heat together soup, cheese, and margarine until melted. Slice potatoes in small slices. Put half in casserole. Add half of the asparagus, half of the soup mixture, and 1 egg. Repeat layers, ending with sliced egg. Parmesan cheese is tasty on top. Bake at 350° until hot.

Pauline Hopper, Illinois

GREEN RICE CASSEROLE
(Broccoli)

Cook 1 cup raw rice in boiling water 20 minutes. Drain.

1 medium onion, chopped
1 c. finely cut celery
1 can cream of mushroom soup
2 boxes frozen chopped broccoli (or
  2 c. fresh, chopped)

Salt and pepper to taste
1 small can mushrooms

Saute onion and celery in ½ cup butter. Add liquid from drained mushrooms into onion and celery mixture. Do not brown. Cook broccoli as package directs. Mix all together while warm: Drained rice, celery-onion mixture, and drained broccoli. Add the mushroom soup, salt, pepper, and mushrooms. Mix. Bake until thoroughly hot in covered casserole.

LaVaine Novak, Nebraska

CREAMED ONIONS

2 lb. whole yellow onions (golf ball
   size)
2 Tbsp. butter
2 Tbsp. flour
1 c. milk

1/3 tsp. salt
1/4 tsp. fresh ground pepper
1/4 c. shredded Cheddar cheese
1/2 c. cracker crumbs

Boil peeled onions until tender. Drain and cool. Melt butter in fry pan. Add flour and stir until bubbly. Add milk and stir until roux is thickened. Add salt, pepper, and cheese. Pour in casserole. Sprinkle with cracker crumbs. Bake at 350° for 30 minutes. Serves 5 to 6. *So good.*

Marilyn Denny, Minnesota

CABBAGE CASSEROLE

2 medium onions, chopped
1 medium size green pepper,
   chopped
1/2 c. butter, melted
2 medium heads cabbage, chopped,
   cooked, and drained

2 1/2 c. shredded Cheddar cheese,
   divided
1 c. bread crumbs
Salt and pepper to taste
1 c. half & half

Saute onions and green pepper in butter in small skillet. Combine with cabbage, 2 cups cheese, bread crumbs, salt, and pepper in large mixing bowl. Pour in large 3 quart casserole. Sprinkle with 1/2 cup cheese. Pour half & half over top. Bake at 350° for 30 to 40 minutes. Serves 10 to 12.

Betty J. Scott, Missouri

BAKED ONIONS

3 c. cooked sliced onions, well
   drained
1 1/2 c. cubed Velveeta cheese
4 slices toasted bread, cubed

1 beaten egg
1 c. milk (I used canned milk)
1 tsp. salt
1/4 tsp. pepper

Combine onions, bread (cubed), and cheese in alternate layers. Pour liquid over and bake at 375° for 30 minutes. *Very good.*

D.E. Adams, Iowa

BROCCOLI AND CAULIFLOWER BAKE

1 (10 oz.) pkg. frozen broccoli,
   chopped (or fresh)
1 (10 oz.) pkg. frozen cauliflower (or
   fresh)
1 (8 oz.) jar Cheez Whiz

1 can cream of mushroom soup
1 can cream of celery soup
1 can milk
7 oz. box Minute rice
1 can sliced water chestnuts

Cook broccoli and cauliflower al dente. Mix rest of ingredients in 2 quart saucepan and heat till bubbles. Put the broccoli and cauliflower in a 2 quart baking dish. Pour cheese and soup mixture over the top and bake at 350° for 45 minutes.

Judy Kleiss, Iowa

ZUCCHINI CASSEROLE

Boil together for 15 minutes or until tender:

2 medium zucchini, peeled and cut into ½ inch slices

1 c. sliced carrots

Drain well. Saute ½ cup chopped onion in 4 tablespoons margarine.

Stir in:

2 c. Stove Top herb stuffing
1 can cream of chicken soup

½ c. sour cream

Gently stir this mixture into the vegetables. Pour into casserole. Melt 2 tablespoons margarine and mix with 1 cup Stove Top herb stuffing. Sprinkle over top of casserole. Bake, covered, in a 350° oven for 35 minutes.

Katherine Deremo, South Dakota

SCALLOPED CORN

2 c. creamed corn
2 eggs, beaten
½ to 1 tsp. salt
Dash of pepper

½ c. soda cracker crumbs
2 Tbsp. butter
¾ c. milk

Combine corn, beaten eggs, salt, pepper, and cracker crumbs. Add milk and put in 2 quart greased casserole. Dot with butter. Bake, uncovered, for 30 to 40 minutes at 350°F.

Mrs. Kenneth Amundson, Iowa

CHEESY HASH BROWN CASSEROLE

2 lb. hash browns, shredded
½ c. butter, melted
1 tsp. salt
1½ tsp. pepper

1 can cream of chicken soup
1 pt. sour cream
¼ c. chopped onion
10 oz. cheese (Cheddar or Velveeta)

Mix butter, salt, pepper, soup, sour cream, onion, and cheese, then mix with thawed hash browns. Bake at 350° for 45 minutes in a 9x13 inch baking dish.

Dana Spurgeon, Missouri

BROCCOLI SUPREME

2 (10 oz.) pkg. frozen chopped broccoli
1 can cream of mushroom soup
1 c. grated Velveeta cheese
2 eggs, beaten

1 c. mayonnaise
2 Tbsp. chopped onion
Salt and pepper to taste
1 c. cheese cracker crumbs

Cook broccoli 5 minutes and drain well. Combine with rest of ingredients, except cracker crumbs. Spread crackers over top and bake at 400° for 30 minutes in a 2 quart casserole. Serves 10.

Charlotte Nelson, Minnesota

Main Dishes

MEAT ROASTING GUIDE

Cut	Weight Pounds	Approx. Time (Hours) (325° oven)	Internal Temperature
BEEF			
Standing Rib Roast [1] (10 inch) ribs)	4	1¾	140° (rare)
[1] If using shorter cut (8-inch)		2	160° (medium)
ribs, allow 30 min. longer		2½	170° (well done)
	8	2½	140° (rare)
		3	160° (medium)
		4½	170° (well done)
Rolled Ribs	4	2	140° (rare)
		2½	160° (medium)
		3	170° (well done)
	6	3	140° (rare)
		3¼	160° (medium)
		4	170° (well done)
Rolled rump [2]	5	2¼	140° (rare)
		3	160° (medium)
		3¼	170° (well done)
Sirloin tip [2]	3	1½	140° (rare)
[2] Roast only if high quality.		2	160° (medium)
Otherwise, braise.		2¼	170° (well done)
LAMB			
Leg	6	3	175° (medium)
		3½	180° (well done)
	8	4	175° (medium)
		4½	180° (well done)
VEAL			
Leg (piece)	5	2½ to 3	170° (well done)
Shoulder	6	3½	170° (well done)
Rolled Shoulder	3 to 5	3 to 3½	170° (well done)

POULTRY ROASTING GUIDE

Type of Poultry	Ready-To-Cook Weight	Oven Temperature	Approx. Total Roasting Time
TURKEY	6 to 8 lbs.	325°	2½ to 3 hrs.
	8 to 12 lbs.	325°	3 to 3½ hrs.
	12 to 16 lbs.	325°	3½ to 4 hrs.
	16 to 20 lbs.	325°	4 to 4½ hrs.
	20 to 24 lbs.	300°	5 to 6 hrs.
CHICKEN (Unstuffed)	2 to 2½ lbs.	400°	1 to 1½ hrs.
	2½ to 4 lbs.	400°	1½ to 2½ hrs.
	4 to 8 lbs.	325°	3 to 5 hrs.
DUCK (Unstuffed)	3 to 5 lbs.	325°	2½ to 3 hrs.

NOTE: Small chickens are roasted at 400° so that they brown well in the short cooking time. They may also be done at 325° but will take longer and will not be as brown. Increase cooking time 15 to 20 minutes for stuffed chicken and duck.

MAIN DISHES

SWEET AND SOUR LAMB

Broil lamb chops or use leftover lamb roast, cut in small chunks. Mix together sweet and sour sauce from store with medium can of crushed pineapple and a teaspoon of soy sauce.

Heat and then add chunks of lamb. Heat through and serve.

You can add small pieces of orange slices or small pieces of green pepper if desired.

Nancy Hamilton, Kansas

LAMB MEATBALLS

1 lb. ground lamb
1 egg, beaten
1/3 c. fine dry bread crumbs
   (Pepperidge Farm dressing mix
   works well)
1/4 c. parsley, chopped

1 tsp. salt
1/4 tsp. lemon pepper
Dash of garlic powder
2 Tbsp. chopped chives or green
   onion tops

Mix well. Shape into 1 inch balls. Brown and cook in skillet. A small amount of butter may be added to start with. Keep fat drained off.

Nancy Hamilton, Kansas

KRISTIE'S MEATBALLS

1 lb. hamburger
3/4 c. oatmeal
1 egg
Onion

1/2 c. milk
Salt
Pepper

Sauce:

3 Tbsp. vinegar
3/4 Tbsp. Worcestershire sauce
1 Tbsp. brown sugar

1/2 c. ketchup
1/2 c. water

Shape ingredients into balls and brown. Mix together sauce and pour over meatballs. Bake at 350° for 1 hour.

Kristie Reierson, Iowa

BEEF 'N' TATER CASSEROLE

1 lb. ground beef
1 can golden mushroom soup
1 can French fried onions

1 (1 lb.) pkg. frozen tater tots
Velveeta cheese

Brown ground beef until beef is no longer pink. Drain. Place in a greased 9x9 inch baking dish. Spoon mushroom soup over beef and spread evenly. Layer with sliced Velveeta cheese until covered. Sprinkle with fried onions and top with frozen tater tots. Bake at 375° for about 15 to 20 minutes until tater tots are golden brown and cheese is melted.

Marcella Doggett, Iowa

"STEW JEWELEAN"

1 lb. ground beef
2 Tbsp. butter
1 medium large onion, chopped
5 medium-size potatoes
4 medium-size carrots
3 large stalks celery

1½ tsp. salt
¼ tsp. pepper
½ tsp. oregano
1 lb. can green beans
1 can cream of mushroom soup

Lightly brown meat. Add onions to meat. Cook until golden. Add potatoes and carrots (cut into strips), and celery (chopped up). Place vegetables over beef. Add seasonings and cover. Simmer until vegetables are barely tender (15 minutes). Add beans and soup and cook 15 minutes more. Serve with salad and a dessert.

I usually brown the meat and onions, then add all the rest of ingredients and simmer until vegetables are done. Any leftover stew is good reheated in microwave oven.

Eva R. Johnson, South Dakota

SALISBURY STEAK

1 can mushroom soup
1½ lb. ground beef or turkey
½ c. dry bread crumbs
½ tsp. salt
⅛ tsp. pepper
¼ tsp. oregano

¼ tsp. basil
1 onion, finely chopped
1 egg, beaten slightly
½ c. water
1 can mushrooms (optional)

In a bowl, combine ¼ cup of soup and all remaining ingredients, except water. Mix well. Shape into 6 patties. Arrange in 13x9 inch dish. Bake, uncovered, at 350° for 20 minutes. Skim off fat. Remove from oven. Combine remaining soup and ½ cup of water. Spoon over patties and bake for 10 more minutes. Serve with noodles, rice or mashed potatoes. Good on hamburger buns too.

Bernese Henderson, Iowa

FAST ITALIAN SKILLET MEAL

1 lb. hamburger
1½ to 2 c. macaroni
1 (46 oz.) can tomato juice

1 Tbsp. Italian seasonings
Sour cream (if desired)
Onion (optional)

Brown beef. Add tomato juice and macaroni. Stir well. Simmer, adding water if needed, about 30 minutes. Can add tomato sauce or canned tomatoes at any time. Serve with sour cream and hot garlic bread.

Katy Bauer, Kansas

SPAGHETTI SAUCE

1 large can crushed tomatoes and 1 can water
2 tsp. sugar
2 tsp. parsley flakes
2 tsp. oregano (or to taste)
1 (12 oz.) can tomato paste and 1 can water

2 lb. ground chuck, browned with chopped onion to taste
1 lb. pork sausage links, cut in fourths and browned
Salt, pepper, and garlic salt to taste

In large pan, place 5 ingredients and water. Brown meats and drain off all grease. Add to tomato mixture. Cook at least 1 hour or more on simmer. Add salt, pepper, and garlic salt. Cook to desired thickness. Add a can of mushrooms if desired. Serve with spaghetti and Parmesan cheese.

Mrs. Dorothy Pfingsten, Illinois

YOO SOON'S MARINATED STEAK

$\frac{1}{2}$ green pepper, slivered
1 medium onion, sliced thin
2 cloves garlic, minced
4 carrots, slivered
2 green onions, cut diagonally
$1\frac{1}{2}$ lb. top round steak, cut diagonally very thin

$\frac{1}{2}$ tsp. Accent
$\frac{1}{4}$ tsp. black pepper
6 Tbsp. soy sauce
1 Tbsp. sugar

Toss all together. Refrigerate in covered container overnight. In electric fry pan, add 4 tablespoons oil and heat to 400°, stir-frying. Serve immediately over a bed of fluffy white rice. Serves 6.

Adeline Dicker, North Dakota

MEXICAN PIE

Press 1 package of crescent rolls into 10 inch pie plate. Bake at 350° to a light golden brown. Remove from oven. While crust is baking, stir-fry 1 pound hamburger and 4 tablespoons chopped onion until lightly browned. Drain grease.

Add:

1 (8 oz.) can tomato sauce
1 pkg. mild taco seasoning mix

1 small can mushrooms, drained and chopped

Spread this mixture in baked crust. Top with 1 cup sour cream and bake for about 15 minutes until cream sets. Remove from oven and top with 8 ounces package of shredded Mozzarella cheese. Return to oven until cheese melts.

Ruth Heck, Iowa

BEEF SUMMER SAUSAGE

2 lb. lean ground beef
1 c. water
1 tsp. liquid smoke
2 Tbsp. Morton's Tender-Quick
   tenderizing salt
1/2 tsp. onion salt

1/4 tsp. garlic salt
2 Tbsp. brown sugar
1/8 tsp. nutmeg
1 tsp. mustard seed (optional)
3 sheets heavy-duty foil (18 inches
   long)

Mix ground beef, water, and liquid smoke together in a large bowl until well blended. Mix other ingredients together and sprinkle over meat mixture. Stir well. Divide into 3 portions and place on 3 sheets of aluminum foil, each 18 inches long. Shape rolls 12 inches long. Roll up in the foil and pinch ends closed. Refrigerate 24 hours. The next day, place on a wire rack in a shallow pan and bake 1 hour at 350°. Cool 10 minutes in foil, then unwrap and cool thoroughly. Store in refrigerator in plastic wrap. Freezes well.

Florence Johnson, Iowa

E-Z MICRO-MEAT LOAVES

1 lb. ground beef
1/2 c. quick oatmeal
1 egg
1 tsp. chili powder
1/2 tsp. salt
1 (8 oz.) can tomato sauce

1 (4 oz.) can chopped green chilies,
   drained
1/4 tsp. garlic salt
4 tsp. minced onion (dried)
1 c. grated medium Cheddar cheese

Combine first 5 ingredients, plus 1/4 cup tomato sauce, 2 tablespoons green chilies, and 3 teaspoons onion. Mix well and shape into 4 loaves. Place in baking dish. Microwave on HIGH for 6 minutes. Turn dish every 2 minutes. Mix garlic salt, remaining tomato sauce, green chilies, and onion in glass bowl. Microwave on HIGH for 1 minute. Spoon sauce over meat loaves and top with grated cheese. Serves 4.

Bev Clauson, Iowa

ZIPPY MEAT BALLS

1 1/2 lb. ground beef
3/4 c. oatmeal
1/2 c. milk

1 small onion, chopped
1 1/2 tsp. salt

Sauce:

1 c. catsup
1/4 c. white vinegar
4 Tbsp. brown sugar

1/2 c. water
1/2 c. chopped onion
2 Tbsp. Worcestershire sauce

Mix all of meat, oatmeal, milk, onion, and salt together. Make into small balls and brown. Mix sauce ingredients; simmer for 5 minutes. Pour over meat balls and bake for 1 hour at 350°.

These can be made ahead and frozen. Bake when wanted. Can also be microwaved for 20 minutes.

Marcella Johnson, Iowa

HOBO HOTDISH

Potatoes, sliced
1/4 c. rice (uncooked)
1 can mushroom soup
1 can tomato soup
1 lb. hamburger (raw)

Carrots, sliced
1 c. milk (may substitute 1/2 c. water
   and 1/2 c. milk)
Salt and pepper to taste

In greased casserole, put layers of potatoes, rice, onion, carrots, hamburger, salt, and pepper. Mix soups and milk and pour over all ingredients. Bake at 350° for 2 to 2 1/2 hours.

Gen Marty, Minnesota

MICROWAVE TACO RICE HOT DISH

1 lb. ground hamburger
1 onion, chopped
1 (16 oz.) can tomatoes
1 c. instant rice (not cooked)

1 pkg. taco seasoning
1 c. Cheddar cheese, shredded
2 c. shredded lettuce

Brown hamburger and onion. Drain tomatoes (save this juice). Add water so you have 2 1/2 cups liquid. Take an 8 x 11.5 x 2 inch microwave or glass dish. Put hamburger, onion, rice, tomato pieces, and taco seasoning in. Mix a little. Add your 2 1/2 cups liquid. Microwave till rice is done! If it seems dry, add some more water. When done, put your shredded cheese and lettuce on top and serve. Serves 6. *Very good.*

Christena Gasner, Minnesota

HAMBURGER CUPCAKES

1 lb. hamburger
1 can mushroom soup
1/4 c. onion
1 egg, beaten

1/2 c. Cheddar cheese, shredded
1/2 c. bread crumbs
Season to taste

Combine ingredients. Trim crust off of 16 to 18 buttered bread slices. Place buttered side down into a cupcake tin. Shape and fill full with meat. Bake at 350° for 40 minutes.

Good cold. Freezes well. Warm in microwave. Use your favorite cheese or bread. Garnish with pickle, radish, olives or whatever.

Marge Koffler, North Dakota

CAVATINI CASSEROLE

1/2 pkg. each 3 different pastas
1 large stick pepperoni, sliced
1 green pepper, diced
1 onion, diced
1 small can tomato paste
1 (15 oz.) can tomato sauce

3 (6 oz.) pkg. Mozzarella cheese
1 can mushrooms
1 pkg. spaghetti sauce mix
1 1/2 lb. hamburger
1 c. water or less

Brown hamburger, onions, and peppers; drain. Season with salt and pepper. Add sliced pepperoni and mushrooms. Add tomato paste, tomato sauce, seasoning

493-95

mix, and water. Cook pastas and add to sauce. Top with cheese. Bake at 350° for 30 minutes in a 9x13 inch pan.

Linda Peterson, Minnesota

GANG'S FAVORITE

Brown and simmer 1½ pounds ground beef ½ hour.

Add:

**1 can cream of chicken or
   mushroom soup
1 can tomato soup**

**1 can sliced carrots
5 or 6 medium potatoes, peeled and
   chopped**

Bake at 350° for 30 minutes (covered). Add 1½ cups frozen peas. Bake 30 minutes longer.

Pat Gjersvik, Minnesota

TERIYAKI STEAK

**1½ c. red wine (not real sweet)
⅓ c. soy sauce
½ c. molasses**

**1 Tbsp. garlic powder (not garlic
   salt)**

Mix the preceding and let stand. Cut sirloin steak into 2 inch wide strips. Marinate at least 3 hours, preferably overnight. Cook on outdoor grill over medium low heat, basting often with marinade.

This can also be used with chicken, pork, or other cuts of beef.

Cliff Smith, Missouri

CAVATINI

**1 lb. ground beef
1 lb. mild ground pork sausage
1 medium onion, chopped
1 green pepper, chopped
1 (3½ oz.) pkg. pepperoni slices,
   chopped
1 (28 oz.) can crushed tomatoes
1 (26½ oz.) can spaghetti sauce
1 (16 oz.) jar mild salsa**

**1 (4 oz.) can sliced mushrooms,
   drained
1 (10 oz.) jar pepperoncini salad
   peppers, drained and sliced
1 (16 oz.) pkg. shell macaroni,
   cooked
1 c. grated Parmesan cheese
4 c. (16 oz.) shredded Mozzarella
   cheese**

Cook ground beef and next 3 ingredients in a large skillet over medium heat, stirring until meat browns and crumbles. Drain well; set aside. Combine chopped pepperoni and next 5 ingredients in a large bowl; stir in meat mixture and pasta shells.

Spoon half of the mixture into 2 lightly greased 11 x 7 x 1½ inch baking dishes; sprinkle with Parmesan and Mozzarella cheese. Top with remaining pasta mixture. Bake at 350° for 30 minutes or until heated. Top with remaining cheeses. Bake 5 minutes.

36

Unbaked casseroles may be frozen up to 3 months (freeze topping cheeses separately). Thaw in refrigerator 24 hours. Let stand at room temperature 30 minutes. Bake at 350° for 40 minutes; sprinkle with cheese. Bake 5 minutes.

Ken and Gail Root, AgriTalk

BLUE CHEESE MEAT LOAF

1 medium onion, chopped
¼ c. chopped green pepper

2 Tbsp. butter

Saute 5 minutes.

Add:

¼ c. chili sauce

2 Tbsp. water

Cook 3 minutes. Pour into bottom of loaf pan, then make topping.

Topping:

1½ lb. ground chuck
¼ c. chili sauce
¼ c. sweet sausage
½ tsp. dry mustard
⅛ tsp. pepper

¼ tsp. sage
2 c. finely chopped bread crumbs
2 eggs
¾ c. (3 oz.) Blue cheese

Bake at 350° about 1 hour. Serves 6 to 8.

Ila Nyman, Illinois

TASTY MAIN DISH CASSEROLE

1½ lb. hamburger
1 onion
1 can cream of celery soup
1 can cream of mushroom soup

1 can water
1 lb. drained sauerkraut
2½ c. uncooked noodles
2 c. grated mild Cheddar cheese

Brown hamburger and onion. Put ½ into a 2½ quart casserole. Mix the soups and water. Put the drained sauerkraut on top of meat, then put the drained noodles on the sauerkraut. Cover with rest of meat mixture. Pour soup mixture over all. Poke holes so soups go down. Cover casserole and bake 1 hour in a 350° oven.

Remove from oven and sprinkle the cheese over. Return to oven another 15 minutes, uncovered, or until cheese is melted. Serve and enjoy.

Mrs. Orin Wangen, Minnesota

HAMBURGER STROGANOFF

1 lb. ground beef
1 medium onion
¼ c. butter
2 Tbsp. flour
1 tsp. salt
1 c. sour cream

1 clove garlic
¼ tsp. pepper
Mushrooms
Cream of chicken soup
2 c. cooked noodles

Cook and stir ground beef and onion in butter till brown and tender. Stir in flour, salt, garlic, pepper, and mushrooms. Cook, stirring constantly, for 5 minutes.

Stir in soup. Reduce heat and simmer, uncovered, 10 minutes. Stir in sour cream. Heat through. Serve over noodles. Serves 4.

Lanette Henry, Texas

BOR-BA-COA

2 to 3 lb. roast
Garlic powder
4 oz. can chilies, diced
Cumin (small amount)
Salt

Pepper
Oregano
1½ c. water
16 oz. picante sauce

Cook first 8 ingredients in crock pot overnight or on stove until tender (3 to 5 hours). Cool; shred meat with fork (first remove all fat and bone if any). Add picante sauce.

Suzie Carroll, Texas

GREEK MEATBALLS

2 lb. hamburger
1 large onion, chopped fine
1 egg
2 Tbsp. Parmesan or Romano
   cheese

1½ tsp. oregano
4 slices bread (crumbs)
½ c. milk
4 oz. tomato sauce
Salt and pepper

Place all ingredients in bowl and blend well. Set in refrigerator for 3 or 4 hours. Shape into small balls. Roll in flour and fry in hot oil until golden brown. They may be baked if desired. May be served hot or cold. Yield: 150 small balls.

Mary Berger, South Dakota

ROSIE'S TACO HOT DISH

1½ lb. hamburger, browned
1 onion, sliced

1 (15 oz.) tomato sauce
1 pkg. taco seasoning mix

Simmer this mixture for 10 minutes. Line the bottom of a 13x9 inch dish with crescent rolls. Sprinkle with 1 cup crushed taco chips. Spread with hamburger mixture. Top with 1 large tub sour cream. Sprinkle with 1 large package shredded Cheddar cheese and top with 1 cup taco chips. Bake at 375° for 25 minutes.

Linda Peterson, Minnesota

HAMBURGER CHOP SUEY CHOW MEIN

1 lb. lean ground beef
½ bunch celery
½ large onion, browned with meat
   (size of onion depends on the
   persons liking of onions)

1 can tomato soup
1 can mushroom soup
1 can chow mein noodles

Mix ½ can chow mein noodles into mixture before baking. Sprinkle the remaining ½ can on top. Celery should be cut and cooked a short time before adding to mixture. Bake 1 hour in moderate oven.

Lois L. Gray, Iowa

RAISED MEATBALLS

4 slices bread
½ c. milk
2 beaten eggs
1½ lb. lean ground beef

¾ tsp. salt
¼ tsp. fresh ground pepper
2 Tbsp. chopped onions
1 tsp. baking powder

Soak bread in milk. Mash and add beaten eggs, ground beef, spices, and baking powder. Mix well and form into 1½ inch balls. Brown in fry pan. Drain. Add to spaghetti sauce or to your favorite sweet and sour recipe. You can also pour on cream of mushroom and cream of chicken soups. Bake till done. Serves 6 to 8.

Marilyn Denny, Minnesota

"QUICK AND EASY" CASSEROLE

And very good, too! Our family favorite.

½ lb. wide noodles
1 lb. ground beef
¼ c. chopped onion
1 c. cubed Velveeta cheese
1 egg, beaten

1 can cream of chicken soup
1 can cream of mushroom soup
½ soup can milk
Soda crackers and margarine

Cook noodles till tender, then drain. Meanwhile, brown ground beef and onion. Drain and add to noodles. Also add beaten egg, soups, milk, and cheese. Combine lightly and pour into 2½ quart casserole. Top with finely crushed cracker crumbs and dot with thin slices of margarine. Bake, uncovered, for 30 to 40 minutes at 350°. Serves 6 to 8.

Variations: Omit ground beef and onions. Add cold, cooked, cubed roast beef, ham, chicken or turkey.

Patricia Jones Baumler, Iowa

BEEF-BURGERS

1 c. finely chopped onions
4 Tbsp. butter
4 lb. ground chuck
1 (14 oz.) bottle ketchup
1 c. water
½ c. chopped celery

¼ c. lemon juice
2 Tbsp. brown sugar
1 Tbsp. Worcestershire sauce
1 Tbsp. salt
2 tsp. vinegar
½ tsp. dry mustard

Saute onions in butter, then brown ground chuck. Drain. Add all other ingredients to beef mixture; simmer slowly for 1 hour. Works well to put in slow cooker on LOW. Serves around 30 to 40 small buns.

Lynn Pestotnik, Iowa

CAVATINI

1 lb. ground beef
½ lb. ground pork
1 (12 oz.) pkg. rotini macaroni
1 (32 oz.) jar spaghetti sauce
1 (4 oz.) can mushrooms

¼ c. taco sauce
2 c. (8 oz.) shredded Mozzarella
    cheese
Italian seasoning (optional)

Brown meats and drain. Boil water for macaroni; cook, then drain. Combine meats, spaghetti sauce, taco sauce, and seasoning. Add macaroni and mushrooms. Mix well. Place in a greased 9x13 inch pan. Sprinkle Mozzarella cheese on top to cover. Bake at 350° for 30 minutes. Let stand a few minutes, then serve.

Jeanne Woll, Iowa

SLOPPY JOES
(Served at the Fremont County Fair)

Brown 5 pounds ground beef and 1 large onion. Drain grease from meat.

Add:

1/2 to 3/4 c. brown sugar
5 c. tomato juice
1 1/4 c. catsup
2 Tbsp. mustard

1 Tbsp. salt
1 tsp. pepper
2 c. quick oatmeal

Simmer 30 minutes.

This can be divided into portions and frozen.

Lois Whitehead, Iowa

BARBEQUED STEAK

Have on hand 4 pounds round steak, cut 1/2 inch thick.

Sauce:

1 c. catsup
1/2 c. water
1/4 c. vinegar
1/4 c. green pepper, chopped
1/4 c. onion, chopped

1 1/2 Tbsp. Worcestershire sauce
1 Tbsp. prepared mustard
2 Tbsp. brown sugar
Salt and pepper

Combine all ingredients in a saucepan. Bring to a boil and simmer 5 to 10 minutes. Pound the steak and cut into serving size pieces. Place in a baking pan, then pour the hot sauce over meat and cover tightly. Bake in a 350° oven for 1 1/2 hours or until meat is tender. Remove cover from pan 10 to 15 minutes before serving.

This recipe can be cut in half.

Lois Whitehead, Iowa

YUMMIE FARMERS CASSEROLE

1 lb. ground beef (lowfat)
1 c. onion, chopped
1 (10 1/2 oz.) can condensed cream of
     mushroom soup
1/2 tsp. Beau Monde seasoning
     (optional)
1/4 tsp. seasoned pepper

1 tsp. seasoned salt
1 c. dairy sour cream
2 tsp. cooking sherry (optional)
2 c. frozen peas
1 (7 oz.) pkg. macaroni
1/4 c. grated cream cheese (optional)

Cook macaroni according to directions. Combine beef, onion, and seasoning in pan. Saute. May be made into 16 meat balls. Brown in small amount of oil. Stir in soup; cover and simmer about 10 minutes. Remove from heat. Stir in sour cream, macaroni, and peas. Pour into 2½ quart casserole. Bake at 350° for 35 minutes. Top with shredded cheese for decoration.

Serve with a tossed salad, rolls, and coffee and dessert if desired.

Bertha Traver, Iowa

TACO PIE

Put 1 can crescent rolls in pie tin and pinch seams. Brown 1 pound hamburger.

Add:

1 (8 oz.) tomato sauce　　　　　**1 pkg. taco seasoning**

Spoon into shell and spread 1 cup sour cream on top of mixture.

Sprinkle:

1 c. crushed Doritos chips　　　　**8 oz. shredded Cheddar cheese**

Top with more crushed chips. Bake at 375° for 25 minutes. May top with lettuce, tomatoes, and hot sauce.

Brenda Kovar, Minnesota

IMPOSSIBLE TACO PIE

1 lb. ground beef　　　　　　　　**1¼ c. milk**
½ c. chopped onion　　　　　　　**¾ c. Bisquick**
1 env. taco seasoning mix　　　　**3 eggs**
1 can chopped, drained green　　**2 sliced tomatoes**
　chilies　　　　　　　　　　　　**1 c. cheese**

Heat oven to 400°. Grease pie pan. Cook and stir 1 pound ground beef and ½ cup chopped onion until brown. Drain. Add 1 envelope taco seasoning mix. Spread in pan. Top with 1 can chopped, drained green chilies. Beat 1¼ cups milk, ¾ cup Bisquick, and 3 eggs for 15 seconds in blender or 1 minute with mixer. Pour into pie pan. Bake 25 minutes. Top with 2 sliced tomatoes and 1 cup cheese. Bake 8 to 10 minutes.

Opal Good, California

LOW CALORIE HOT DISH

1 small head cabbage　　　　　　**1 can tomato soup***
1 lb. hamburger　　　　　　　　　**1 soup can water***
1 small onion, chopped　　　　　**1 Tbsp. brown sugar***
⅓ c. rice (uncooked)　　　　　　**1 tsp. lemon juice**

Brown meat and onion; drain off fat. Add raw rice and mix. Mix tomato soup, water, brown sugar, and lemon juice. Heat to boiling. Chop cabbage in medium size pieces and place in greased 1½ to 2 quart oblong baking dish. Spread hamburger and rice mixture over cabbage. Cover all with tomato soup mixture. Bake in preheated 350° oven for at least 1 hour. Cover dish with foil while baking to keep moisture in.

This recipe can be made using sausage, pork chops, etc.

Can microwave also. Microwave 15 to 17 minutes for smaller casserole and 20 to 25 minutes for larger casserole at MEDIUM power. Check for cabbage and rice doneness. Cover dish with Saran Wrap "vent" to keep in moisture.

* Season with salt, pepper, or other spices to taste.

Jannivie Czajkowski, Illinois

SHEPHERD'S PIE

Brown 1 pound hamburger with ½ chopped onion. Add salt and pepper to taste. Drain.

Crust:

2 c. Bisquick   **½ c. cold water**

Mix and press into 9x13 inch pan. Add hamburger and ½ pound Cheddar cheese. Top with 4 servings of mashed potatoes. Sprinkle with parsley. Bake at 350° for 40 minutes, uncovered.

Missy Etzenhouser, Kansas

BEEF SKILLET FIESTA

1 lb. ground beef	**1 (1 lb.) can tomatoes**
¼ c. diced onion	**1 (12 oz.) can whole kernel corn**
2 tsp. salt	**1¼ c. beef broth (Swansons)**
1 tsp. chilli powder	**½ c. thin strips green pepper**
Pepper	**1⅓ c. Minute rice**

Brown 1 pound ground beef; add ¼ cup diced onion and cook until tender, but not brown. Add 2 teaspoons salt, 1 teaspoon chilli powder, pepper, 1 can tomatoes, 1 can whole kernel corn, and 1¼ cups beef broth. Add ½ cup thin strips green pepper. Boil again. Add 1⅓ cups Minute rice. Remove from heat. Cover. Let stand 5 minutes and serve.

Wanda Earp, Texas

WHEAT CHILI

1½ c. wheat kernels	**⅛ tsp. cayenne pepper**
4 c. water	**⅛ tsp. black pepper**
2 lb. lean ground beef	**1 (8 oz.) can tomato sauce**
1 large onion, chopped	**1 (16 oz.) jar medium salsa**
1 green pepper, chopped	**4 c. beef broth**
1 tsp. salt	**1 (15 oz.) can kidney beans**
½ tsp. garlic powder	**1 (4 oz.) can mushroom pieces**
1 Tbsp. chili powder	

Cook wheat in water for 1 hour until tender; add more water if necessary. Drain and rinse with cool water. Brown beef, onion, and pepper. Drain off fat thoroughly. Stir in remaining ingredients. Simmer, uncovered, 1 hour or until desired consistency is reached. Stir occasionally. Garnish with shredded cheese of your choice.

Mrs. LaVerne Stecher, North Dakota

YUMMY BEEF BALLS

1 pkg. dry onion soup
2 eggs

2 lb. ground chuck

Sauce:

6 oz. can sauerkraut
¾ c. chili sauce
1 (8 oz.) can cranberry sauce with
    whole berries

⅓ c. brown sugar

Mix soup, eggs, and ground chuck together. Form into small balls, 1½ inches, then slightly brown on all sides in skillet. Mix sauce ingredients together in bowl. Put ½ of sauce in bottom of 9x13 inch pan, then set meat balls on sauce. Pour the rest of the sauce over top. Cover with foil and bake at 325° for 20 minutes. Uncover and bake 20 minutes. Serves 8 to 10.

Lynn Pestotnik, Iowa

TORTILLA CASSEROLE

1 lb. lean ground meat, browned
1 can Ro-Tel tomatoes with chilies
1 can cream of mushroom soup

1 can cream of chicken soup
12 tortillas
1½ c. grated cheese

Combine first 4 ingredients in large bowl. Using a large Pyrex casserole dish, line the bottom with tortillas torn into pieces. Pour half of soup mixture over tortillas. Cover with half of the grated cheese. Make another layer of tortillas. Add the rest of the mixture and top with tortillas and cheese. Bake, uncovered, in a 375° oven for 25 minutes.

Rebecca Norris, Minnesota

WINTER PRESSURE COOKER STEW

Cut 2 pounds meat into 1½ inch pieces and roll in flour, salt, and pepper. Brown in cooker.

Add:

2 onions, sliced
3 large carrots (¾ inch pieces)

3 stalks celery (¾ inch pieces)
2 large potatoes (1 inch pieces)

Toss lightly.

Pour in:

2 (12 oz.) cans V-8 juice

2 c. water (or until cooker is ⅔ full)

Add:

1 tsp. salt

¼ tsp. pepper

Close the cover and bring the pressure to 15 pounds. Cook for 10 minutes. Remove to sink and run cold water over it until able to open.

Nancy Schlindwein, Iowa

HAMBURGER PIE

Flatten a roll of Ballard biscuits into a pie pan, making a pie shell; set aside. Brown 1 pound hamburger with a little onion in skillet. Pour in a can of drained vegetables and a can of cream of something soup. Stir and pour into pie shell, then cover with slices of Velveeta cheese. Bake in 350° oven just until biscuits are baked, 10 to 12 minutes. *Yum. Yum!*

Velma Williams, Illinois

BEEF STROGANOFF

Here is my favorite recipe:

6 Tbsp. flour
2 lb. round steak, cut into squares
1/2 c. butter or Crisco
1 medium onion, chopped
2 cans mushrooms or more
    (depending on how well you like
    them)

1/2 tsp. Worcestershire sauce
1 1/2 to 2 c. sour cream
1 tsp. salt
1/4 tsp. pepper
2 bouillon cubes (beef)

Pound flour into steak, cut into bite-size pieces. Brown in butter and take meat out of skillet. Add onions and mushrooms. Cover and simmer 5 minutes. Put meat back into pan. Add sauce and cream. Cover and reheat to boiling. Serve over cooked rice or mashed potatoes. I use part milk instead of all cream for reducing calories.

Mrs. Raymond Klein, North Dakota

QUICK BEEF CASSEROLE

1 lb. ground beef
1 onion, chopped
Salt to taste
Pepper to taste

16 oz. can green beans
1 can Cheddar cheese soup
Tater tots

Brown beef with onion. Season with salt and pepper. Drain off any excess fat and place in 8x8 inch baking dish. Drain beans and pour over meat mixture. Pour soup over top. Top with layer of tater tots. Bake at 350° about 45 minutes.

Janet Gorman, Iowa

FAVORITE POT ROAST

Combine:

1 tsp. seasoning salt
1/2 tsp. onion powder

1/4 tsp. pepper
1/8 tsp. garlic powder

Rub on a 3 to 4 pound beef chuck pot roast. Brown roast in 1 tablespoon oil in skillet. Place in roasting pan.

Add:

3/4 c. water
1 large onion, chopped
1/4 c. chopped green pepper
2 cloves garlic, chopped

2 bay leaves
2 tsp. dried parsley flakes
1/4 tsp. dried thyme

Cover and bake 2½ to 3 hours at 325°.

Mrs. Leon Koopman, Nebraska

ENCHILADA CASSEROLE

12 frozen corn tortillas
1½ lb. hamburger
½ medium green pepper, chopped
1 Tbsp. chili powder
1 lb. Velveeta cheese

1 can cream of chicken soup
2 cans tomatoes with green chilies,
   drained
1 can chili beans

Line a 9x13 inch pan with 6 tortillas. Brown hamburger with green pepper, chili powder, and salt and pepper to taste. Pour over tortillas. Pour on chili beans. Put in ½ pound Velveeta cheese. Put on 6 more tortillas. Mix soup in tomatoes. Pour over tortillas. Cover with rest of cheese. Bake at 350° for 30 to 45 minutes. *Delicious!!*

Sheryl Waters, Iowa

EASY AND QUICK POLISH SURPRISE

1 lb. hamburger
1 lb. sausage (hot or mild)
1 lb. Velveeta cheese

1 tsp. garlic powder
1 tsp. oregano
Party rye bread

Brown meat and drain off grease. Mix in cheese, garlic powder, and oregano until cheese is melted. Serve on rye bread.

Marsha Thomas, Indiana

SPECIAL LIVER

1½ lb. sliced liver
2 onions, peeled and sliced
1 Tbsp. reduced sodium soy sauce

1 Tbsp. beef base
½ c. water

Brown liver in small amount of grease. Season with pepper (no salt). Drain any grease from liver. Reduce heat. Mix together soy sauce, beef base, and water. Pour over liver and add onions. Cover and cook until liver is tender. Serves 4.

I came up with this to give the liver a beefier taste.

Peg Fast, South Dakota

LIVER AND ONIONS

Slice liver ¼ inch thick. Roll in flour and brown in hot shortening. Turn over and place 1 slice of onion on each piece of liver. Salt and pepper, then pour tomato juice over till liver is almost covered. Put lid on pan and simmer over low heat for about 30 minutes.

I also add a few small potatoes to cook with it.

Gladys Tinker, Iowa

PRONTO SPICY BEEF AND BLACK BEAN SALSA
(First place)

Total preparation and cooking time: 40 minutes.

1 beef tri-tip (bottom sirloin) roast *or* top sirloin steak, cut 1½ inches thick

1 (15 oz.) can black beans, rinsed and drained

1 medium tomato, chopped

1 small red onion, finely chopped

3 Tbsp. coarsely chopped fresh cilantro

Fresh cilantro sprigs (optional)

Seasoning:

1 Tbsp. chili powder

1 tsp. ground cumin

1 tsp. salt

½ tsp. ground red pepper

1. Combine seasoning ingredients; reserve 2 teaspoons for salsa. Trim fat from beef roast. Press remaining seasoning mixture evenly into surface of roast.

2. Place tri-tip on grid over medium coals (medium-low coals for top sirloin). Grill tri-tip 30 to 35 minutes (top sirloin 22 to 30 minutes) for rare to medium doneness, turning occasionally. Let stand 10 minutes before carving.

3. Meanwhile, in medium bowl, combine beans, tomato, onion, chopped cilantro, and reserved seasoning mixture; mix until blended.

4. Carve roast across the grain into slices. Arrange beef and bean salsa on serving platter; garnish with cilantro sprigs if desired. Makes 6 servings (252 calories per ⅙ of recipe).

Cook's tips: To check the temperature of coals, cautiously hold the palm of your hand about 4 inches from the coals. Count the number of seconds you can hold your hand in that position before the heat forces you to pull it away - 4 seconds for medium coals and 4 to 5 seconds for medium-low coals.

To broil tri-tip, place roast on rack in broiler pan so surface of roast is 4 to 5 inches from heat. Broil 25 to 30 minutes for rare to medium doneness, turning once.

Recipe reprinted by permission from the National Beef Cook-Off sponsored by the American National CattleWomen and in cooperation with the Beef Industry Council.

Sylvia Harber, Boulder City, Nebraska

CHILI SALSA BEEF
(Second place)

Total preparation and cooking time: 1¾ hours.

1½ lb. boneless beef chuck shoulder roast

1 Tbsp. olive oil

1 c. prepared medium *or* hot chunky salsa

2 Tbsp. packed brown sugar

1 Tbsp. reduced-sodium soy sauce

1 clove garlic, crushed

⅓ c. coarsely chopped fresh cilantro

2 Tbsp. fresh lime juice

2 c. cooked rice

Cilantro sprigs (optional)

1 lime, cut crosswise into quarters (optional)

1. Trim fat from beef roast. Cut roast into 1¼ inch pieces. In Dutch oven, heat oil over medium heat until hot. Add beef and brown evenly, stirring occasionally. Pour off drippings if necessary.

2. Stir salsa, sugar, soy sauce, and garlic into beef. Bring to a boil; reduce heat to low. Cover tightly and simmer 1 hour. Remove cover and continue cooking, uncovered, an additional 30 minutes or until beef is tender.

3. Remove from heat; stir in chopped cilantro and lime juice. Spoon beef mixture over rice; garnish with cilantro sprigs and lime quarters if desired. Makes 4 servings (446 calories per ¼ of recipe).

Recipe reprinted by permission from the National Beef Cook-Off sponsored by the American National CattleWomen and in cooperation with the Beef Industry Council.

Robert Logan, Garnett, Kansas

CALYPSO STEAK
(Third place)

Total preparation and cooking time: 35 minutes. Marinating time: 20 minutes to 2 hours.

1½ lb. boneless beef top sirloin *or* top round steak, cut 1 inch thick

Edible flowers (optional)

Marinade:

½ **medium onion, cut into quarters**	**1 to 2 jalapeno peppers, stems removed and cut in halves**
¼ **c. honey**	**3 cloves garlic, peeled**
¼ **c. fresh lime juice**	½ **tsp. ground allspice**
¼ **c. soy sauce**	½ **tsp. ground paprika**
10 to 20 quarter-size slices peeled fresh ginger, cut from 1 inch wide x 1½ to 3 inch long piece	½ **tsp. dried thyme leaves**

1. Place marinade ingredients in blender or food processor, fitted with steel blade; process until blended. Place beef steak and marinade in plastic bag, turning to coat. Close bag securely and marinate in refrigerator 20 minutes to 2 hours, turning once.

2. Remove steak from marinade; reserve marinade. Place steak on rack in broiler pan so surface of meat is 3 to 4 inches from heat. Broil top sirloin 16 to 21 minutes (top round 15 to 18 minutes) for rare to medium doneness, turning once.

3. Meanwhile, in small saucepan, bring reserved marinade to a rolling oil over high heat. Boil 2 minutes; strain and set aside for sauce.

4. Trim fat from steak. Carve steak crosswise into thin slices; arrange on serving platter. Garnish with edible flowers if desired; serve with sauce. Makes 6 servings (229 calories per ⅙ of recipe).

Recipe reprinted by permission from the National Beef Cook-Off sponsored by the American National CattleWomen and in cooperation with the Beef Industry Council.

Robin Bonifay Hill, Arlington, Texas

REUBEN BAKE

1 (16 oz.) can drained sauerkraut
8 oz. sliced corned beef (can break
   into pieces)
1/4 c. rye cracker crumbs
1 tsp. caraway seed

2 medium tomatoes, sliced
1/2 c. Thousand Island dressing
2 c. grated Swiss cheese
1 Tbsp. butter or oleo

Layer sauerkraut, beef, tomatoes, dressing, and cheese in a 1 1/2 quart casserole or dish. Bake at 375° for 15 minutes. Remove from oven. Combine crumbs, butter, and seeds. Mix until crumbly. Sprinkle crumb mixture on baked ingredients and then add cheese on top. Bake 15 minutes longer until bubbly and hot. Can cut into squares. Serve hot.

Norma Schaaf, Iowa

CANTONESE DINNER

1 1/2 lb. pork steak (1/2 inch thick), cut
   into strips
2 Tbsp. oil
1 large onion, sliced
1 small green pepper, cut in strips (I
   use frozen peppers - out of
   season)

1 (4 oz.) can mushrooms, drained
8 oz. can tomato sauce
3 Tbsp. brown sugar
1 1/2 Tbsp. vinegar
1 1/2 tsp. salt (or less)
2 tsp. Worcestershire sauce

Brown pork strips in oil in skillet to remove excess fat. Drain on double paper towels. Place pork strips and all remaining ingredients in crock pot. Cover and cook on LOW for 6 to 8 hours (HIGH 4 hours). Serve over hot fluffy rice.

Patricia Wells, Missouri

PORK PINWHEEL

2 lb. lean ground pork
1 c. dry bread crumbs
2 eggs, slightly beaten
1/3 c. milk
1/2 tsp. salt
1/4 tsp. pepper
1 tsp. thyme leaves, crushed

1 Tbsp. Worcestershire sauce
1 (16 oz.) can sauerkraut, drained
   and finely cut
1/2 c. chopped onion
1/2 c. chopped pimento
3 Tbsp. sugar
5 slices bacon

Combine and mix together pork, bread crumbs, eggs, milk, salt, pepper, thyme, and Worcestershire sauce. Chill 1 hour.

Meanwhile, combine sauerkraut, onion, pimento, and sugar. On waxed paper, pat pork mixture into a 9x12 inch rectangle. Spread sauerkraut mixture over meat. Roll up from narrow end. Place loaf in a greased large loaf pan or baking dish. Lay bacon slices on top (long way). Bake in a 350° oven about 1 hour and 10 minutes. Makes 8 servings.

Mrs. Evert Meyer, Minnesota

"PORK CHOPS" BAKED

Grease cake pan, 9x13 inches. Spread 1½ cups rice. Put 6 or 8 pork chops on top, then season with Lawry's salt and pepper.

1 can cream of mushroom soup   **1 can mushrooms**
2 cans water   **½ bag dry onion soup**

Bake 2 hours (covered) at 325°.

Can also substitute chicken instead of pork chops.

DeLaine Friedrichs, Minnesota

HEART HEALTHY PORK STIR-FRY

1 lb. lean boneless pork, sliced in ¼   **½ lb. carrots, cut in ⅛ inch diagonal**
** inch thick strips**   ** slices**
1 Tbsp. vegetable oil   **1 Tbsp. low sodium soy sauce**
1 small onion, sliced
1 clove garlic, minced
½ lb. fresh broccoli, stems cut in ⅛
** inch slices and flowerettes**
** separated**

Quickly brown strips in hot oil in wok or large skillet, stirring constantly. Add onion, garlic, broccoli stems, and carrots. Cook until vegetables are hot, but crisp, stirring constantly. Add broccoli flowerettes and soy sauce. Cook and stir 1 minute. Makes 4 servings.

Mary Kermes, Minnesota

BREAKFAST CASSEROLE

1 lb. sausage   **1 c. shredded Cheddar cheese**
1 pkg. Potatoes O'Brien   **8 eggs**

Fry sausage. Remove from skillet when brown. Fry potatoes in sausage grease. When almost done, remove from skillet and mix with sausage in casserole dish or baking pan. Beat eggs and pour over all. Top with cheese and bake until set in middle. Time will depend on size of container. This can also be microwaved on HIGH until set.

Linda Volk, Illinois

PORK CHOPS SUPREME

6 thin Iowa chops (not smoked)   **1½ c. chicken broth**
2 Tbsp. oil   **Salt and pepper**
3 Tbsp. flour   **6 potatoes, peeled and sliced**

Brown chops in oil in heavy skillet, turning once. Remove chops and keep warm. Pour off all but 3 tablespoons drippings from skillet. Sprinkle with flour and cook, stirring until lightly browned. Stir in broth. Bring to a boil, stirring until gravy thickens. Season. Place potatoes in bottom of casserole; pour gravy over chops. Season with salt, pepper, and garlic if you like. Cover. Bake 1½ hours at 350°. Remove cover and bake 20 to 30 minutes longer. Serves 6.

Jan E. Johansen, Iowa

ORANGE AND APPLE PORK CHOPS

4 to 6 center cut pork chops
1 apple
1 orange
½ c. orange juice

1½ Tbsp. brown sugar
1 can beef broth
2 Tbsp. cornstarch

Brown chops. Salt and pepper to taste. Slice orange and apple and place 1 slice of each on each chop. Sprinkle brown sugar over each chop. Pour beef broth over chops. Simmer ½ to 1 hour. Add a little water if necessary.

When ready to serve, remove chops and fruit. Mix orange juice and cornstarch. Slowly add to beef broth. Simmer until thickened. Replace chops and use fruit on top as garnish (fruit usually tastes bitter).

A large electric frypan or large square pan works best.

Pat Gjersvik, Minnesota

SANTA FE CURED PORK LOIN

3 to 4 lb. boneless pork loin roast
8 c. water
1 c. sugar
6 Tbsp. chili powder
2 Tbsp. salt

2 Tbsp. crushed thyme
1 Tbsp. ground cumin
2 tsp. coarsely ground black pepper
2 tsp. crushed oregano

In large saucepan, heat all ingredients, *except* pork loin, to boiling, stirring to dissolve ground spices. Mix cure ingredients thoroughly. Remove from heat and cool to room temperature. Place pork loin in glass container large enough to immerse roast in cure solution; cover and refrigerate 2 to 4 days. *Or,* place roast in 2 gallon self-sealing plastic bag and pour cure solution over; seal bag and place in large bowl. Refrigerate 2 to 4 days.

Remove pork roast from cure, discarding cure solution. Pat pork gently dry with paper towels. Prepare covered grill with banked coals heated to medium-hot. Place roast over drip pan and cook over indirect heat for 45 minutes to an hour, until thermometer inserted reads 155°F. to 160°F. Remove from grill and slice to serve. Makes 12 servings.

Preparation time: 20 minutes. Cooking time: 60 minutes.

Nutrition information per 3 ounce serving: 181 calories, 133 mg sodium, 24 g protein, 66 mg cholesterol, and 6 g fat.

Reprinted with permission from the National Pork Producers Council.

GRILLED PORK ROAST WITH PEPPER JELLY GLAZE

Have 4 pound pork loin roast, rolled and tied.

Marinade:

1 c. apple juice
1 c. cider vinegar

1 c. hot pepper jelly

Glaze:

¾ c. pepper jelly

¼ c. cider vinegar

Place pork in large Ziploc bag. Heat marinade ingredients together until jelly melts; pour over pork in bag. Seal bag and refrigerate 12 to 24 hours.

Prepare covered grill with banked coals. Remove pork from marinade, reserving marinade. Place pork roast over drip pan and cover grill. Grill pork for about 1¼ hours, until thermometer inserted in center reads 150°F., basting occasionally with leftover marinade. Stir together glaze ingredients; coat roast with jelly glaze for last 10 minutes of grilling, bringing roast to an internal temperature of 160°F. Let rest 10 to 15 minutes before slicing to serve. Makes 16 servings.

Preparation time: 10 minutes. Cooking time: 90 minutes.

Nutrient information per 3 ounce serving: 160 calories, 60 mg sodium, 24 g protein, 66 mg cholesterol, and 6 g fat.

Reprinted with permission from the National Pork Producers Council.

ROAST PORK LOIN SOUTHWEST STYLE

4 lb. boneless pork loin roast, trimmed
1 Tbsp. olive oil
2 medium tomatoes, chopped and seeded (about 2 c.)
1 medium onion, chopped (about 1 c.)
½ c. chopped fresh cilantro
1 tomatillo, peeled and chopped (about ⅓ c. - optional)

4 cloves garlic, minced
1 jalapeno pepper, chopped and seeded (optional)
1 (4 oz.) can chopped green chilies, drained
½ tsp. dried oregano leaves
½ tsp. ground cumin
½ tsp. ground red pepper
½ tsp. ground coriander

Heat oil in a large skillet over medium heat. Add tomatoes, onion, cilantro, tomatillos, garlic, jalapeno pepper, and chilies; cook about 2 minutes or until onion is tender, stirring frequently. Add oregano, cumin, red pepper, and coriander; mix well. Refrigerate mixture until thoroughly chilled.

Heat oven to 325°F. Spray shallow baking pan with nonstick cooking spray. Using sharp knife, cut 8 to 10 slits about 1 inch long and 1 inch deep in top and sides of pork roast. Press heaping teaspoonful of cold vegetable mixture into each slit; spread remaining mixture over top and sides of roast. Place in prepared pan. Roast for about 1½ hours, or until meat thermometer registers 155°F. Let stand 10 minutes before slicing. Makes 16 servings.

Preparation time: 15 minutes. Cooking time: 90 minutes.

Nutrient information per 3 ounce serving: 180 calories, 133 mg sodium, 26 g protein, 66 mg cholesterol, and 7 g fat.

Reprinted with permission from the National Pork Producers Council.

GREEN CHILE BURRITOS

2 lb. lean pork, ground or diced
3 (10½ oz.) cans chicken broth
2 (7 oz.) cans chopped mild green chiles
1 (16 oz.) can tomatoes, chopped
12 large white flour tortillas

2 (16 oz.) cans refried beans
Flour
2 c. grated Cheddar cheese (8 oz.)
3 c. shredded lettuce
3 tomatoes, chopped
Chopped onion

Simmer pork in broth until tender and thoroughly cooked. Add chiles and canned tomatoes. Simmer 15 to 20 minutes longer. Spread each tortilla with refried beans. Using a slotted spoon, put some pork mixture on each tortilla, reserving liquid to serve as sauce. Roll each tortilla and place in a shallow greased baking dish. Bake, uncovered, at 350° for 15 minutes or until hot.

Thicken sauce with a little flour and spoon over burritos. Serve topped with grated Cheddar, shredded lettuce, chopped tomatoes, sour cream, etc.

Marilyn Cowell, Missouri

BAKED NOODLES AND PORK CHOPS

6 pork chops
Mustard
8 oz. pkg. noodles

½ onion, chopped
2 cans cream of chicken soup
2 cans water

Brown pork chops on one side. Remove to platter, brown side up. Spread with mustard. Cook noodles and drain. Place in 9x13 inch pan. Arrange chops, mustard side down, on top of noodles. To drippings in skillet, saute onion. Add soup and water. Stir until smooth. Pour over chops. Bake ½ hour covered and ½ hour uncovered at 350°.

Kristie Reierson, Iowa

PORK CHOPS WITH STUFFING

Marinate pork chops in Italian dressing overnight. Brown and put in pan.

Stuffing: Brown 1 pound of pork sausage. Saute ¼ cup minced onion and ½ cup chopped celery in ⅓ cup margarine. Mix with pork sausage. Add ½ teaspoon sage, ½ teaspoon thyme, and 4 cups croutons. Add water to moisten. Cover pork chops with stuffing. Bake at 325° for 1 hour. Bake, covered.

JoAnn Boettcher, Iowa

HAM LOAF

1½ lb. ground ham
½ lb. ground pork
2 eggs, beaten slightly
½ c. milk

1 c. soft bread crumbs
1 tsp. dry mustard
2 Tbsp. chopped onion
⅛ tsp. black pepper

Combine all ingredients. mix well. Grease a 9x5 inch loaf pan. Place all ingredients in pan. Bake at 350° for 1 hour. Makes 1 (2 pound) loaf. Slice and serve. Serves 8 people.

Margaret Horstman, Kentucky

IOWA STUFFED PORK CHOPS

6 to 8 pork chops (1 to 1¼ inches
    thick)
8 slices bread
2 eggs
1 tsp. sage
1 small onion

Salt and pepper (to taste)
2 tsp. melted butter
½ c. brown sugar
1 tsp. mustard
½ tsp. Worcestershire sauce
⅓ c. ketchup

Make pocket in each chop parallel to bone side. Mix bread, eggs, sage, onion, salt and pepper, and butter (melted) for stuffing. Stuff each pocket of chop. Fasten with toothpick. Wrap in foil. Cook on grill 15 to 20 minutes on each side. Remove foil. Make a sauce using ketchup, brown sugar, mustard, and Worcestershire sauce. Brush on chop. Turn and brush other side. Serve. *M-m good.*

The man that gave this recipe took first prize at country fair and went on to Iowa State Fair.

Marjorie Cox, Iowa

OVEN BAKED BREADED PORK CHOPS

4 lean pork chops (about ¾ inch
    thick)
1 c. fine dry cracker or bread
    crumbs
1 Tbsp. grated Parmesan cheese
¼ tsp. powdered thyme

½ tsp. paprika
⅛ tsp. garlic salt
1 tsp. Lawry's seasoning salt
¼ c. soft butter
1 egg, slightly beaten

Combine crumbs and seasonings. Blend in soft butter with fork or pastry blender. Dip chops in egg, then in crumbs, patting in crumbs lightly. Place chops on a wire rack in a 15x10x1 inch jellyroll pan lined with foil. Bake at 375° for 50 to 60 minutes. Turn once after baking 30 minutes.

Grace Rasmussen, Minnesota

AMERICAN-CHINESE CASSEROLE

1 lb. ground chuck or lean ground
    pork
3 stalks celery, chopped
1 small onion, chopped
1 can cream of mushroom soup
1 can cream of chicken soup
1 c. Minute rice

1 can mushrooms (optional)
½ c. milk
½ c. water
1 Tbsp. soy sauce
Pepper
1 can chow mein noodles

Brown meat, onion, and celery together till celery is quite tender. Add all other ingredients, except the chow mein noodles. Put in casserole (greased or sprayed with Pam). Bake at 350° for 20 to 30 minutes. Put chow mein noodles on top and bake 10 minutes more.

Mrs. Dorothy Pfingsten, Illinois

APRICOT HAM BALLS

1 (1 lb. 14 oz.) can apricot halves
1 lb. ground ham
1/2 lb. ground beef (lean)
1 lb. sausage
2 eggs
1 c. bread crumbs
1/4 c. finely chopped onion

1/8 tsp. pepper
1 c. packed brown sugar
1/4 c. vinegar
2 Tbsp. flour
1 tsp. prepared mustard
1/2 tsp. Worcestershire sauce

Combine ham, beef, sausage, eggs, bread crumbs, onion, pepper, and 3/4 cup syrup and blend well. Roll into either meal size meat balls or, if using for buffet, into smaller balls. Place balls side by side in a 9x13 inch glass cake pan or similar pan. Bake in a 325° oven for 30 minutes. I turn them over after one side is brown and brown other side.

While these are baking, mix sugar, flour, vinegar, mustard, Worcestershire sauce, and 1/2 cup apricot syrup in bowl (glass). Microwave these ingredients until thick, stirring often. Remove meat balls to another container and cover with the glaze. Pour the glaze over the meat balls and the apricot halves and bake another 25 to 30 minutes at 325°. *Easy and good.*

Note: Meat balls may be frozen after the first baking of 30 minutes and then can be used later.

Rosalie Nelsen, Nebraska

SWEET AND SOUR PORK

1/2 c. all-purpose flour
1/2 tsp. salt
1 lb. lean pork, cut in 3/4 inch cubes
1 well-beaten egg
1/2 c. sugar
1/2 c. vinegar
1/3 c. pineapple juice
1/4 c. catsup

1 tsp. soy sauce
2 Tbsp. cornstarch
2 Tbsp. cold water
1 c. pineapple chunks, drained
1 medium green pepper, cut in 1/2
   inch pieces
Hot cooked rice

Combine flour and salt. Dip pork chops in beaten egg, then in flour mixture, coating each piece well. Fry pork in deep hot fat (360°) till browned and done, about 6 to 8 minutes. Drain on paper toweling; keep warm.

In wok or deep skillet, combine sugar, vinegar, pineapple juice, catsup, and soy sauce; bring to boiling. Blend cornstarch with cold water; gradually stir into pineapple juice mixture. Continue cooking, stirring constantly, till mixture is thickened and bubbly.

Stir warm pork cubes, drained pineapple chunks, and green pepper pieces into thickened sauce. Heat, stirring constantly, till mixture is heated through, about 5 minutes. Serve with rice. Makes 3 or 4 servings.

Maleta Breamer, Minnesota

BOHEMIAN SWEET SOUR CABBAGE, PORK, AND DUMPLINGS

1. Cook 2 1/2 to 3 pounds lean pork roast for 3 1/2 to 4 hours at 300°. Watch and add a little water and turn to 250° if getting too brown.

2. Cut 1 large head (or 2 small heads) cabbage into small pieces. Season with salt, pepper, and caraway seed. Cook in small amount of water in large kettle, covered (about 1 to 1½ hours).

3. Brown 2 medium sliced onions in butter in a small skillet.

4. Dumplings:

1½ c. sifted flour	2 eggs and milk to make a total of
2 tsp. baking powder	¾ c. liquid
¾ tsp. salt	

Stir only until blended. Drop by heaping spoonfuls onto the cooking cabbage about 20 minutes before it is done. Cook for 10 minutes uncovered and then 10 minutes covered (do not lift lid). Place on top of food to cook (not in liquid). Makes 6 to 8 dumplings.

5. Remove dumplings to serving dish. Pour most of the water from the cabbage.

Add:

½ c. vinegar	¼ c. flour (enough to thicken)
1 or 2 Tbsp. sugar	Browned onions
Juice from the roast (1 c. or less if greasy)	

Cook and stir until thickened. Serve over cut up dumplings with the pork roast.

The Bohemian cabbage and dumpling recipe is an old one also, from my husband's grandmother. She and her husband emigrated from Czechoslovakia early in the century and farmed for many years in the Schuyler, Nebraska area.

Linda Marek, Iowa

PORK CHOP CASSEROLE

You can adjust this recipe by how many people will be eating. Brown pork chops or pork steak in small amount of shortening, just enough to keep from burning. Put into a large casserole. Top with fresh sliced potatoes, a drained can of green beans, and fresh onion slices. Put into the frying pan about ½ cup of warm water and stir until most of the little bits in the frying pan are loose. Add 1 can of cream of mushroom soup and heat thoroughly and pour over the casserole. Put into 350° oven and bake for at *least* 2 hours. It is even better the second day.

Nancy Schlindwein, Iowa

CROCK POT SCALLOPED POTATOES AND HAM

5 or 6 potatoes, peeled and sliced	1 can cream of celery soup
1 small onion, diced	4 slices boneless ham
1 c. shredded Cheddar cheese	1 c. milk
1 carrot, shredded	

Mix potatoes, onion, cheese, carrot, and soup. Add milk. Mix and place in lightly greased 3½ quart crock pot. Top with ham slices. Cook 8 to 10 hours on LOW. May wish to cover ham with some of the potato mixture as it tends to dry on the top. Serves 4 to 6.

Linda Marek, Iowa

SUPER HAM AND RICE CASSEROLE

1/3 c. salad oil
1 c. onion, chopped
3/4 c. green pepper, chopped
3/4 c. uncooked rice
1 tsp. salt

1/2 tsp. pepper
1 (No. 21/2) can tomatoes
2 c. cooked ham, diced
1 can pitted ripe olives, drained
1 small bay leaf

Mix all ingredients together, then pour into a greased 2 quart casserole. Cover and bake in a moderate 350° oven for 1 hour and 15 minutes, stirring occasionally. Remove bay leaf before serving. Serves 4 to 6 nicely.

Mrs. Bertha Traver, Iowa

HAM LOAF

2 lb. cured ham, ground
1 lb. fresh pork, ground
2 eggs, well beaten

1/2 c. catsup
1 c. crushed corn flakes
6 crackers, rolled

Mix all together.

Top with paste made of:

1 Tbsp. flour
1 Tbsp. mustard

1 Tbsp. water

Bake in loaf pan 15 minutes at 350° and 45 to 60 minutes at 325°.

Betty Seidt, Missouri

MARINATED PORK TENDERLOIN

2 pork tenderloins (about 2 lb.)
4 tsp. soy sauce
1 tsp. brown sugar

4 Tbsp. dry sherry
1 tsp. ginger
3 garlic cloves, crushed

Trim any excess fat from pork tenderloins. Place marinade in 11x7 inch glass dish and tenderloins on top. Cover and refrigerate for at least 1 hour. Grill with medium heat for 10 to 15 minutes on each side. Grill potatoes, red pepper, and zucchini also if desired.

Pour reserved marinade into small saucepan. Mix 1 teaspoon cornstarch in 1/2 cup water. Add to sauce and heat to boiling. Remove and pour in bowl.

Place tenderloins on cutting board and cut in 1/2 inch slices. Arrange on platter. Serve with sauce. Arrange vegetables if desired. Can be broiled inside or baked.

Carole Burke, Iowa

SAUSAGE CASSEROLE

1 lb. pork sausage, browned
4 to 6 oz. noodles
1 can cream of chicken or cream of
    mushroom soup
1/2 c. milk
1 Tbsp. pimento
1 Tbsp. green pepper

1/4 c. celery
Onion
1 c. shredded cheese
1/2 c. soft bread crumbs, buttered (3
    or 4 slices) and croutons
    sprinkled with sage

Brown sausage and drain off grease. Cook noodles as directed. Combine all ingredients. I cover casserole for 30 minutes with foil. Put buttered croutons on top the last 10 to 15 minutes. If I double recipe, I use 1 chicken soup and 1 mushroom soup. Bake at 350° for 40 minutes.

Alberta Shevel, Iowa

PORK CHOPS SCALLOPED POTATOES

Brown 6 pork chops on one side in hot oil. Place 2½ cups sliced peeled raw potatoes in a greased baking dish. Top with 6 slices process American cheese. Add 2½ cups more potatoes. Place pork chops browned side up on potatoes. Sprinkle with 1 teaspoon salt and some pepper. Cook ½ cup chopped green onions in drippings in skillet until tender. Do not brown. Add 1 can condensed cream of celery soup and 1¼ cups milk. Heat. Pour over pork chops. Cover with foil and cook at 350° for 1 hour. Remove cover and bake 30 minutes more or until potatoes are tender. *Delicious.*

Mary Ann Cappo, Kansas

CHICKEN SANTA FE

Cook 4 medium potatoes in microwave until tender, about 8 to 10 minutes. Cut in ¾ inch cubes. Cut 1 large boned skinned chicken in ¾ inch cubes.

2 Tbsp. oil   **1 small can drained corn**
1 c. tomato salsa

Toss chicken in a skillet in oil until brown, about 5 minutes. Add potatoes and saute lightly until brown. Add salsa and corn. Toss and heat thoroughly for about 20 minutes. Serves 4.

Contains 340 calories and 9 grams fat.

Shirley Wellik, Iowa

PHEASANT WITH WILD RICE

2 c. cooked wild rice   **½ soup can milk**
1 onion, finely chopped   **1 c. grated Cheddar cheese**
1 can cream of mushroom soup   **2 pheasants, cut in pieces**

Heat mushroom soup and milk. Add cheese. Add to wild rice and onion. Roll pheasant in flour and brown. Pour rice mixture into greased casserole. Top with pheasant. Sprinkle with paprika. Cover and bake at 325° for 1 hour.

Rita Nietfeid, Minnesota

CHICKEN CHALUPA CASSEROLE

8 small flour tortillas   **1 pt. sour cream**
4 chicken breasts, cooked and   **¾ lb. Monterey Jack cheese**
** cubed**   **1 onion, grated**
2 cans cream of chicken soup   **¾ lb. grated Cheddar cheese**
1 small can diced green chilies

Combine soup, chilies, onion, sour cream, Jack cheese, and chicken. Grease a 9x13 inch baking dish. Cut tortillas in halves and layer with Cheddar cheese and soup mixture. Sprinkle with paprika. Refrigerate overnight. Bake at 350° for 45 minutes.

Cathy Evans, Texas

LOW CHOLESTEROL CHICKEN

In skillet, brown 2 deboned chicken breasts, skin removed, in 2 tablespoons corn oil or safflower oil. Drain and transfer to baking dish. Brown ½ onion, chopped, in same skillet. Stir 1 tablespoon flour and ¼ package Italian dressing mix into skillet. Add 8 ounces tomato sauce. Cook until thickened. Add 1 tablespoon sugar and one 10 ounce package frozen mixed vegetables. Pour over chicken. Cover and bake in 350° oven for 1 hour. Skim fat.

Ellen Adams, Minnesota

TURKEY ON THE GRILL

Use 13 pound turkey and aluminum foil roaster.

2 onions, sliced   **1 lemon, quartered**
3 apples, quartered

Put half in turkey and the other half in an aluminum roaster around turkey. Lay 6 slices of bacon across breast of turkey.

Sauce:

3 sticks oleo, melted   **½ c. honey**
½ c. brown sugar   **½ c. wine**

Mix together and pour over turkey. Cover roaster with foil. Baste every ½ hour. Grill for ½ hour on high and 3 hours on low.

Cleo Wiskus, Iowa

TURKEY OR CHICKEN CASSEROLE

Boil chicken or use leftover turkey or baked chicken. Take off bone and tear into bite-size pieces. Place in bottom of greased baking dish.

Mix together:

2 cans cream of chicken soup   **1 c. chicken broth**
1 small can evaporated milk

Mix until smooth and pour over chicken or turkey. Mix 1 small package Pepperidge Farm stuffing with some chopped onion, chopped celery, 1 egg, and 1 cup chicken broth. Pour over soup and meat mixture. Bake 45 minutes in a 350° oven.

Marilyn Cowell, Missouri

PRESBYTERIAN CHURCH'S CHICKEN CASSEROLE

1 c. macaroni (uncooked)   **1 egg, boiled and chopped**
2 cans cream of chicken soup   **¼ c. Cheddar cheese, grated**
¾ c. milk

Mix together. Cover and refrigerate overnight. Bake at 350° for ½ hour.

Sometimes I adjust this recipe by using 1 can chicken soup and 1 cup milk.

Lois Whitehead, Iowa

CRISPY SUNSEED CHICKEN

¼ c. cornstarch
2 tsp. salt
1 tsp. sugar
1½ Tbsp. dry sherry (water may be
    substituted)
2 egg whites

1¼ c. finely chopped sunflower
    seeds
2 whole chicken breasts, skinned,
    boned, and thinly sliced
2 c. sunflower seed oil

In a small bowl, combine cornstarch, salt, sugar, and sherry. In separate bowl, beat egg whites lightly until just frothy. Gradually add cornstarch mixture. Stir gently until blended. Place chopped sunflower seeds on plate. Dip chicken slices into egg mixture and then coat with sunflower seeds. Place chicken pieces on waxed paper or plate.

Pour oil into deep fryer or wok. Heat oil, uncovered, over medium to medium high heat until it reaches 375°. Drop 4 to 8 chicken slices carefully into hot oil, using a slotted spoon. Fry until golden brown on all sides, about 2 to 3 minutes. Remove from oil and place on rack or paper towel to drain. Continue frying remaining pieces. (The first may be kept warm in oven.) Makes about 32 appetizers or 6 main dish servings to serve with oriental vegetables or rice.

Ann Berle, North Dakota

HONEY-GLAZED CHICKEN KEBABS

1 pkg. (4 to 6 large) boneless,
    skinless chicken breasts
1 large yellow summer squash
1 large zucchini

2 medium red bell peppers (or 1
    green and 1 red)
6 oz. medium size mushrooms

For glaze:

¾ c. honey
½ c. prepared spicy mustard
2 Tbsp. soy sauce

1 Tbsp. cider vinegar
2 Tbsp. cornstarch
¼ c. water

Prepare coals in grill; place grill rack 6 inches from heat source. Or, preheat oven to 450°. Cut chicken, yellow squash, zucchini, peppers, and mushrooms into bite-size pieces. Thread onto skewers; set aside.

Prepare glaze: In 2 quart saucepan on grill rack or over medium-high heat on stove, bring honey, mustard, soy sauce, and vinegar to boil. In a cup, blend cornstarch with water until smooth. Gradually stir into honey mixture. Bring to a boil; boil 1 minute, stirring constantly, until thickened.

Grill kabobs over medium to medium-hot coals for 8 to 10 minutes, turning often and brushing with glaze until chicken is tender. Or, bake 15 to 20 minutes, turning often, until chicken is tender; continue baking 5 minutes, basting until well-glazed and cooked through. Makes about 6 servings.

MEXICAN CHICKEN

1 large fryer, cooked and boned
1 medium onion, chopped
1 green bell pepper, chopped
1 clove garlic, chopped
1 can cream of mushroom soup

1 can cream of chicken soup
1 can Ro-Tel tomatoes
1/2 lb. Cheddar cheese, grated
12 tortillas

Saute onion and pepper until soft, *not* brown. Add garlic, soups, and Ro-Tel tomatoes and let mixture get hot.

Tear half of tortillas in pieces and layer on bottom of buttered 9x13 inch Pyrex dish. Add 1/2 of soup mixture, half of chicken, and half of cheese. Repeat the layers, using all of the remaining ingredients. Cover with foil and bake at 325° for 30 minutes. Remove cover and add a little extra cheese on top. Return to oven until cheese melts.

E. Jones, Texas

TURKEY OR CHICKEN NOODLES CASSEROLE

4 c. diced chicken or turkey
1 can cream of chicken soup
8 oz. pkg. fine noodles
1 box asparagus tips
1/2 c. chopped celery and onion

1/2 c. mayonnaise
1 medium size green and red
  peppers, diced fine
1/2 c. white cracker crumbs

Cook noodles according to package directions. Drain. Heat together turkey or chicken, soup, and mayonnaise. Stir gently and mix well. Cook celery, onion, asparagus, and pepper till tender; drain.

Put half noodles on bottom of ungreased 2 quart casserole. Cover noodles with celery, onion, pepper, and asparagus. Top with 1/2 chicken or turkey mix. Repeat the layering process. Top chicken with cracker crumbs. Bake in preheated 350° oven for 45 minutes. Serves 10.

Hope you will enjoy this dish.

Anna Mae Welter, Iowa

OKIE-GIRL CHICKEN AND DRESSING

2 c. boiled chicken meat, cut-up
  into small pieces
1 (8½ oz.) pkg. Jiffy corn bread mix
1 pkg. Lipton rice and sauce mix
1 small pkg. Stove Top stuffing mix
  (chicken flavor)
1 large onion, chopped into small
  pieces

1 medium stalk celery, chopped into
  small pieces
1 (10¾ oz.) can cream of chicken
  soup
3 (14½ oz.) cans chicken broth

Cook corn bread according to directions; set aside to cool. After corn bread is cool, mix the following ingredients in an extra large bowl: Chicken, corn bread, Lipton rice and sauce mix, onion, Stove Top stuffing, celery, cream of chicken soup, and chicken broth. Mix all ingredients well. Put into a 13x9x2 inch baking pan. Cook 1 hour and 15 minutes at 400°. Dressing should be lightly browned on top.

Special notes:

Instead of boiling your own chicken, you can buy cooked chicken meat in a can.

You do not prepare the rice and sauce or the stuffing mix according to their directions - simply add the dry ingredients into the bowl.

This is an outstanding meal that serves 8 people anytime of the year for less than $10.00.

Vivian Clapp, Oklahoma

ITALIAN STYLE CHICKEN

4 boneless skinless chicken breasts
1 c. shredded Mozzarella cheese
1 can Italian tomato soup
   (Campbell's)

20 croutons (your choice of flavor),
   crushed

Place chicken in a 9x13 inch baking dish. Sprinkle shredded cheese over chicken. Next, cover mixture with tomato soup. Spread evenly over chicken. Sprinkle crushed croutons over mixture. Bake at 350° for 1 hour.

Judith Woltering, Illinois

CHICKEN CASSEROLE

Mix:

¾ c. mayonnaise
1 tsp. lemon juice
½ tsp. salt

1 Tbsp. minced onion
1 can cream of chicken soup

Add:

1 c. chopped chicken
1 c. cooked rice

3 hard-boiled eggs
1 c. chopped celery

Top with:

¼ c. margarine, melted
1 c. crushed corn flakes

½ c. slivered almonds

Bake 25 minutes at 350° or till hot throughout.

Lois Anderson, Iowa

QUICK AND EASY CHINESE CHICKEN

1 lb. chicken breasts (boneless)
1 pkg. frozen stir-fry vegetables
1 Tbsp. chicken broth granules
1 c. water
Equal parts corn starch and soy
   sauce

3 c. cooked rice
1 Tbsp. oil
¼ tsp. garlic
Salt and pepper to taste

Mix equal parts of corn starch and soy sauce together in mixing bowl. Add cut-up chicken, coating chicken pieces well. Cook chicken in oil on medium heat until done, stirring frequently. Sprinkle with garlic, salt, and pepper. Add water and bouillon granules; stir well. Simmer on low heat 5 minutes. Add entire package of frozen vege-tables to chicken/broth mixture; cook on low until vegetables are done, but not over-cooked. Serve over rice. Makes 2 large servings.

Daunita Cordes, Missouri

SWEET AND SOUR CHICKEN

4 lb. chicken pieces or 2 chickens, cut
1 c. soy sauce
1 tsp. ginger

1 c. sugar
¼ c. oil
1 (8 oz.) can crushed pineapple
½ tsp. garlic salt

Mix preceding and pour over chicken. Let marinate for 6 hours (or overnight). Put in 9x3 inch pan and bake in a 350° oven for 1½ hours. *Delicious.*

Malane Kallenbach, Iowa

STACKI UPPI
(Serve buffet style)

Place in order:

1. Cooked rice.
2. Cubed turkey or chicken.
3. Gravy (equal parts - canned chicken broth and cream of chicken soup).
4. Chinese noodles.
5. Chopped fresh tomatoes.
6. Chopped celery.
7. Grated Cheddar cheese.
8. Chopped green onions.
9. Crushed pineapple.
10. Shredded coconut.
11. Chopped salted peanuts.
12. Sauteed mushrooms.
13. Gravy (chicken broth and cream of chicken soup).

Start with No. 1 and stacki uppi.

Pat Gjersvik, Minnesota

CHICKEN CASSEROLE

4 c. chicken
4 c. celery
1½ c. mayonnaise
1 c. toasted slivered almonds

4 Tbsp. lemon juice
4 tsp. grated onion
1 tsp. salt

Bake chicken first for 1 hour at 350°. Sprinkle with salt, pepper, and garlic. Take off skin after cooking. I use Sam's frozen chicken breasts (skinless, boneless). Pile high in pan. Sprinkle with 1 cup shredded cheese, then 2 cups crushed potato chips. Bake at 425° for 20 minutes in a 9x13 inch pan.

Terri Arnold, Kansas

FULL O' BOLOGNA CASSEROLE

2 lb. bag cubed hash brown
  potatoes (frozen)
1 can undiluted cream of mushroom
  soup
½ soup can milk

1 onion, diced
2 Tbsp. chopped fresh parsley
1 ring bologna
1 c. shredded Cheddar cheese

Place frozen hash browns in large casserole or small roaster. Place diced onion in casserole along with soup and milk. Add parsley and stir to mix. Add cheese. Skin and cube bologna. Add to casserole and mix well. Bake in preheated 350° oven for 1½ to 2 hours. Test to make sure potatoes are tender. Serves 10 to 12.

A sure winner at every picnic. I never bring home leftovers! No one believes the meat is plain old bologna. I never buy the "all beef" or high price - just any bologna on sale!

Marilyn Denny, Minnesota

ONE LARGE SIMPLY PIZZA

1 pkg. active dry yeast
·1 Tbsp. sugar
1 c. lukewarm water
3 c. flour
1 tsp. salt
¼ c. olive oil

1 (15 oz.) can pizza sauce
1 lb. browned hamburger or
  browned ground pork sausage
1 lb. Mozzarella cheese
4 oz. pepperoni slices

Crust: Dissolve yeast and sugar in water. Let rest until foamy, about 15 minutes. Add olive oil. Make a well in the flour and salt. Add yeast and oil mixture. Stir well. Add more flour if dough seems sticky. Knead on floured surface for about 5 minutes until smooth and elastic, adding flour if needed. Pat dough into ball and let rise in a warm place for about 1 hour until doubled. Roll crust into a circle on floured surface. Place on well oiled large pizza pan.

Spread pizza sauce over crust. Spread browned meat over sauce. Top with grated Mozzarella cheese and pepperoni slices on top. Bake for 25 minutes or until crust is browned.

Katy Bauer, Kansas

ALMOST PIZZA

7 c. thinly sliced peeled potatoes
  (about 3 lb.)
1½ lb. lean ground beef
1 (11 oz.) can condensed Nacho
  cheese soup
1 c. milk
1 (10¾ oz.) can condensed tomato
  soup

½ c. chopped onion
1 tsp. salt
½ tsp. dried oregano, crushed
1 (3½ oz.) pkg. sliced pepperoni
1 to 2 c. shredded Mozzarella
  cheese

Place the sliced potatoes in a greased 13x9x2 inch baking dish; set aside. Brown the ground beef and drain off the fat.

Meanwhile, combine cheese soup and milk in small saucepan over medium heat, stirring until heated through. In a mixing bowl, stir together tomato soup, onion, sugar, and oregano. Sprinkle ground beef over potatoes. Pour cheese mixture over all. Top with tomato soup mixture and sliced pepperoni, then Mozzarella cheese. Cover and bake at 350° to 375° for approximately 1½ hours, until potatoes are tender. Let stand 5 minutes before serving. Serves 8 to 10.

Our family and "hunters" love this meal.

Mrs. Kandace Sump, Iowa

PASTA WITH PAZZAZ

½ lb. rigatoni-style pasta
1 pkg. Italian sausage links, cut into
    pieces
1 medium onion, chopped
1 green pepper, chopped
1 can mushrooms
1 tsp. dried basil
1 small can tomato sauce
1 small can tomatoes, chopped
½ tsp. pepper

Cook pasta according to package directions. Set aside; keep warm.

Meanwhile, in a large skillet, cook sausage links 4 to 5 minutes; add onion and green pepper, stirring occasionally, 3 to 4 minutes or until onion is soft. Add basil and tomato sauce; cook 8 to 10 minutes. Stir in the tomatoes and the pepper; cook 3 minutes or until heated through. To serve, place pasta in serving bowl and top with meat mixture.

The original recipe called for a cup of frozen corn kernels. It didn't hurt the taste but it just didn't turn me on.

Nancy Schlindwein, Iowa

BRUNCH PIZZA

1 lb. pork sausage
1 c. frozen hash browns, thawed
    (uncooked)
1 c. shredded Cheddar cheese
5 large eggs
¼ c. milk
⅛ tsp. pepper
2 Tbsp. Parmesan cheese

Crumble sausage in skillet. Cook over medium heat 5 to 7 minutes until cooked through and browned. Remove from skillet; drain excess fat. Spoon into 10 inch pie plate. Top with hash browns and then Cheddar cheese. Beat eggs with milk and pepper. Pour over Cheddar cheese. Sprinkle with Parmesan cheese. Bake 30 to 35 minutes until slightly puffed and knife inserted comes out clean.

This can be made ahead of time if completely wrapped and refrigerated. Reheat at 350° for 20 to 30 minutes.

Marlene Steffan, North Dakota

CRESCENT ROLL PIZZA
(A family favorite)

Brown 1½ pounds ground beef.

Add:

½ env. taco mix   15 oz. can tomato sauce

Cook 5 minutes more. Lay out 1 can crescent rolls in 9x13 inch greased cake pan. Put meat mixture on top of this. Sprinkle 1 cup of grated Mozzarella cheese and

1 cup grated Cheddar cheese over meat mixture. Lay out 1 can crescent rolls over this. Bake 30 minutes at 350° (just till lightly browned). Don't cover.

Barbara Jacobsen, Iowa

BUBBLE PIZZA DISH

Brown 1 pound lean ground beef and onion (optional).

Add:

2½ c. Prego spaghetti sauce
1 can drained mushrooms
⅔ pkg. pepperoni, cut in halves

2 containers (7.5 oz.) raw buttermilk
biscuits, cut in quarters with
scissors

Mix the preceding all together in large bowl. Put in greased 9x13 inch pan. Bake at 400° for 20 minutes.

1 c. grated Cheddar cheese

2 c. Mozzarella cheese

Add on top of the mix in pan. Use no cover. Bake 10 minutes more.

Jean Giese, Wisconsin

FRUIT PIZZA

Crust:

½ c. powdered sugar
¾ c. soft margarine

1½ c. flour

Mix together; pat in pan. Bake at 300° for 10 to 15 minutes (no longer). Cool.

First layer:

1 (8 oz.) pkg. softened cream
cheese

½ c. sugar
1 tsp. vanilla

Beat until creamy. When crust has cooled, spread mixture over top.

Second layer: Arrange any amount of any combination of fruit on top of the cream cheese mixture. Use fruit like strawberries, kiwi, bananas, blueberries, pineapple, oranges.

Glaze:

2½ Tbsp. cornstarch
1 c. fruit juice (pineapple is best)

¾ c. sugar
1 tsp. lemon juice

Heat to a boil. Cook until slightly thickened. Cool and pour over pizza. Eat!

Enjoy your show. Try never to miss it.

Paula Egnoske, Nebraska

SUPER SALMON LOAF

1 can cream of celery soup
⅓ c. mayonnaise
1 egg, beaten
½ c. chopped onion
¼ c. chopped green pepper

1 tsp. lemon juice
1 (16 oz.) can salmon, drained
1 c. cracker crumbs (Keebler club crackers)

Combine all ingredients. Mix well, then place in greased loaf pan. Bake at 350°F. for 40 minutes.

Etta Winter, New York

STUFFED SHELLS

1 lb. tofu, mashed
½ lb. Mozzarella cheese, grated
¼ c. fresh parsley, chopped
2 Tbsp. onion powder
1½ tsp. salt
½ tsp. garlic powder

½ tsp. basil
3½ c. tomato sauce
4 oz. jumbo macaroni shells, cooked
⅓ c. fresh Parmesan cheese

Mix together the tofu, cheese, parsley, onion powder, salt, garlic powder, and basil. Spoon into shells, using approximately ⅓ cup mixture in each shell. Spread 2 cups tomato sauce in the bottom of a 9x9 inch pan. Arrange shells on sauce. Spoon remaining sauce over shells. Sprinkle Parmesan on top of shells. Bake for 25 to 30 minutes at 350°F. until bubbling. Yields 10 shells.

Nutritional value (per serving - 2 shells): 234 calories, 0 g fat, 16 g protein, and 32 g carbohydrates.

Reprinted with permission from the Minnesota Soybean Research and Promotion Council.

FRANKFURTER APPLE BEAN BAKE

¼ c. molasses
3 Tbsp. mustard
2 Tbsp. vinegar
2 tsp. Worcestershire sauce

2 cans baked beans
1 can apple slices
1 lb. frankfurters

Mix together and put in a 2 quart casserole. Bake 45 minutes at 350°.

Margaret Hagemeier, Minnesota

SOUR CREAM ENCHILADAS

1 doz. corn tortillas
½ c. cooking oil
2 c. (8 oz.) shredded Monterey Jack cheese
¾ c. chopped onions (optional)

¼ c. butter
2 c. chicken broth
1 c. dairy sour cream
1 (4 oz.) can chopped green chiles
¼ c. flour

In skillet, cook tortillas, one at a time, in hot oil for a few seconds on each side. (Do not overcook or they won't roll.) Place 2 tablespoons shredded cheese and 1 tablespoon chopped onion on each tortilla; roll up. Place, seam side down, in 11¾ x 7½ x 1¾ inch baking dish.

In saucepan, melt butter. Blend in flour. Add chicken broth; cook, stirring constantly, till mixture thickens and bubbles. Stir in sour cream and peppers. Cook till heated through, but do not boil. Pour over enchiladas. Bake in 425° oven for 20 minutes. Sprinkle remaining cheese. Return to oven for 5 minutes till cheese melts.

Brenda Watkins, Texas

TUNA BAKE

1 can tuna
½ c. celery
¼ c. onion or a little less

1 can mushroom soup
½ c. hot water
1 can Chinese noodles

Bake 45 minutes.

Nellie Smith, Iowa

MEATLESS LOAF

Grind or chop very fine:

1 c. potatoes
1 c. onion
1 c. bread (whole wheat crumbs)

1 c. carrots
1 c. nuts

Mix preceding ingredients.

Add:

2 eggs
1 c. milk

½ can condensed tomato soup
3 Tbsp. melted butter

Add salt and pepper to taste. Bake 1½ hours at 350°. (Use 8x8 inch glass dish.)

Sauce: Make 1 cup medium white sauce. Add remaining ½ can of tomato soup. Use as gravy at serving time. Sprinkle with chopped parsley if desired.

David Sampson, Wisconsin

SCALLOPED SALMON

1 can salmon
1 c. peas and liquid
1 c. cracker crumbs

2 eggs, beaten
1 c. milk (added to eggs)

Mix all well. Potato chips may be placed on top. Bake slowly 1 hour.

Alice Oehler, Wisconsin

CORRINE'S ACCIDENTAL CASSEROLE

2 c. cooked rice
1 (2 inch) onion, diced
1 (16 to 20 oz.) pkg. frozen
    vegetables (broccoli, cauliflower
    mixes are best - cook briefly)

1 (10 oz.) can cream soup (chicken,
    celery or mushroom)
1 (8 oz.) jar *jalapena* Cheez Whiz

Mix rice, onions, and drained veggies in casserole. Melt Cheez Whiz in soup and pour over rice mixture. Stir to blend. Bake at 375° about 40 minutes till good and hot through.

Yes, I accidentally discovered this good spicy taste when I found my grandkids licking the bowl - never have used plain Cheez Whiz since.

Corrine Wessling, Missouri

BAR-B-QUE SHRIMP

This recipe was dreamed up by our daughter while in college. Poor college kids!! It is easy and is the hit of any dinner.

3 sticks butter
2 cloves garlic, minced
Hot sauce to taste (we use a lot)
Paprika
Salt and pepper

1 lime or lemon, sliced
Dash of oregano
1 Tbsp. chili sauce
1 c. white wine
1 lb. raw shrimp in shells

Marinate shrimp for 1 to 3 hours in the sauce made from all the ingredients mixed together. Melt the butter and add everything else. Bake in a 300° oven for 30 minutes or until shrimp turn pink. Don't overcook. Serve with toss salad and crusty French bread and use the sauce in the shrimp to dip bread into.

Rich and Sharon Hull, AgriTalk

CHILI DOGS

½ to 1 small can chopped black
  olives
½ to 1 can chopped chili peppers
1 small onion, chopped

1 (8 oz.) can tomato sauce
½ lb. bologna, ground
½ lb. Velveeta cheese, diced or
  ground

Grind cheese and bologna and mix together. Add olives, peppers, and onion. Add tomato sauce. Fill hot dog buns. Wrap in heavy wax paper or foil and heat in 300° oven about ½ hour. Filling may also be frozen.

Linda Mercado, California

CROCK POT DRESSING

12 c. seasoned croutons (three 8
  oz. bags)
1 stick oleo
1½ tsp. sage
1 onion, diced
½ c. chopped celery
⅓ c. evaporated milk

½ tsp. salt
½ tsp. pepper
1 c. chopped chicken
1 can cream of chicken soup
1 can cream of mushroom soup
1 qt. chicken broth (I use bouillon
  cubes)

Saute sage, celery, and onion in oleo. Mix milk, salt, pepper, chicken, soups, and chicken broth. Add onion mixture and stir. Pour over croutons and mix well. Put in greased crock pot for 1 hour on HIGH, then 5 to 7 hours on LOW till hot all the way through. Or, bake in greased 9x13 inch pan for 45 minutes to 1 hour at 350°.

Cleo Wiskus, Iowa

CORN BREAD DRESSING

2 (8 inch) pans corn bread
10 biscuits
2 large onions
2 stalks celery

6 eggs
5 c. chicken broth
Sage, poultry seasoning, salt,
    pepper

Crumble corn bread and biscuits in a large pan. Add chopped onions and celery and raw eggs. Moisten mixture well with chicken broth and stir all ingredients until well blended. Add sage, poultry seasoning, salt, and pepper to taste. Bake at 400° for 45 minutes. Makes a 9x13 inch pan of dressing.

Pauline Hopper, Illinois

WILD RICE DRESSING

Cook 1 box wild long grain rice as on the box.

Cook until almost done:

1 lb. sausage
1 chopped onion

2 chopped celery

Add 1 small jar of mushrooms. Mix all together. Add 1 can of mushroom or chicken soup. Add 1 egg. Bake at 350° for 40 to 45 minutes or in the crock pot for 3 hours.

Note: I use hot sausage as we like the hot spicy taste.

Janette House, Iowa

Notes

Breads, Rolls

MICROWAVE HINTS

1. Place an open box of hardened brown sugar in the microwave oven with 1 cup hot water. Microwave at high for 1½ to 2 minutes for ½ pound or 2 to 3 minutes for 1 pound.
2. Soften hard ice cream by microwaving at 30% power. One pint will take 15 to 30 seconds; one quart, 30 to 45 seconds; and one-half gallon 45 seconds to one minute.
3. One stick of butter or margarine will soften in 1 minute when microwaved at 20% power.
4. Soften one 8-ounce package of cream cheese by microwaving at 30% power for 2 to 2½ minutes. One 3-ounce package of cream cheese will soften in 1½ to 2 minutes.
5. Thaw frozen orange juice right in the container. Remove the top metal lid. Place the opened container in the microwave and heat on high power 30 seconds for 6 ounces and 45 seconds for 12 ounces.
6. Thaw whipped topping...a 4½ ounce carton will thaw in 1 minute on the defrost setting. Whipped topping should be slightly firm in the center but it will blend well when stirred. Do not overthaw!
7. Soften jello that has set up too hard—perhaps you were to chill it until slightly thickened and forgot it. Heat on a low power setting for a very short time.
8. Dissolve gelatin in the microwave. Measure liquid in a measuring cup, add jello and heat. There will be less stirring to dissolve the gelatin.
9. Heat hot packs in a microwave oven. A wet finger tip towel will take about 25 seconds. It depends on the temperature of the water used to wet the towel.
10. To scald milk, cook 1 cup milk for 2-2½ minutes, stirring once each minute.
11. To make dry bread crumbs, cut 6 slices bread into ½-inch cubes. Microwave in 3-quart casserole 6-7 minutes, or until dry, stirring after 3 minutes. Crush in blender.
12. Refresh stale potato chips, crackers or other snacks of such type by putting a plateful in the microwave oven for about 30-45 seconds. Let stand for 1 minute to crisp. Cereals can also be crisped.
13. Melt almond bark for candy or dipping pretzels. One pound will take about 2 minutes, stirring twice. If it hardens while dipping candy, microwave for a few seconds longer.
14. Nuts will be easier to shell if you place 2 cups of nuts in a 1-quart casserole with 1 cup of water. Cook for 4 to 5 minutes and the nut meats will slip out whole after cracking the shell.
15. When thawing hamburger meat, the outside will many times begin cooking before the meat is completely thawed. Defrost for 3 minutes, then remove the outside portions that have defrosted. Continue defrosting the hamburger, taking off the defrosted outside portions at short intervals.
16. To drain the fat from hamburger while it is cooking in the microwave oven (one pound cooks in 5 minutes on high), cook it in a plastic colander placed inside a casserole dish.
17. Cubed meat and chopped vegetables will cook more evenly if cut uniformly.
18. When baking large cakes, brownies, or moist bars, place a juice glass in the center of the baking dish to prevent a soggy middle and ensure uniform baking throughout.
19. Since cakes and quick breads rise higher in a microwave oven, fill pans just half full of batter.
20. For stamp collectors: place a few drops of water on stamp to be removed from envelope. Heat in the microwave for 20 seconds and the stamp will come right off.
21. Using a round dish instead of a square one eliminates overcooked corners in baking cakes.
22. When preparing chicken in a dish, place meaty pieces around the edges and the bony pieces in the center of the dish.
23. Shaping meatloaf into a ring eliminates undercooked center. A glass set in the center of a dish can serve as the mold.
24. Treat fresh meat cuts for 15 to 20 seconds on high in the microwave oven. This cuts down on meat-spoiling types of bacteria.
25. A crusty coating of chopped walnuts surrounding many microwave-cooked cakes and quick breads enhances the looks and eating quality. Sprinkle a layer of medium finely chopped walnuts evenly onto the bottom and sides of a ring pan or Bundt cake pan. Pour in batter and microwave as recipe directs.
26. Do not salt foods on the surface as it causes dehydration (meats and vegetables) and toughens the food. Salt the meat after you remove it from the oven unless the recipe calls for using salt in the mixture.
27. Heat left-over custard and use it as frosting for a cake.
28. Melt marshmallow creme in the microwave oven. Half of a 7-ounce jar will melt in 35-40 seconds on high. Stir to blend.
29. Toast coconut in the microwave. Watch closely as it browns quickly once it begins to brown. Spread ½ cup coconut in a pie plate and cook for 3-4 minutes, stirring every 30 seconds after 2 minutes.
30. Place a cake dish up on another dish or on a roasting rack if you have difficulty getting the bottom of the cake done. This also works for potatoes and other foods that don't quite get done on the bottom.

BREADS, ROLLS

REFRIGERATOR ROLLS

2 pkg. dry yeast
2½ c. lukewarm water
1 Tbsp. salt
¾ c. sugar
½ c. shortening, melted and cooled

7½ c. bread flour
½ tsp. soda
½ tsp. baking powder
1 egg

Soak yeast in ½ cup lukewarm water for 5 minutes. Dissolve salt and sugar in remaining 2 cups lukewarm water. Add soaked yeast. Add 3 cups flour, sifted with soda and baking powder. Beat well. Add egg and beat again. Add melted shortening. Blend well. Add remaining flour.

Cover securely with damp cloth between 2 sheets of waxed paper and tie over bowl. Place in refrigerator until ready to use. Dough may be kept up to 7 days. When ready to make rolls, remove from refrigerator, punch down, and let stand 20 minutes. Shape into rolls of any desired shape and let rise until doubled. Bake at 400° for 15 to 20 minutes.

Mary Siedschlag, North Dakota

BEST BREAKFAST ROLLS

Soften 1 package dry yeast in ¼ cup warm water in mixing bowl.

Add:

1 tsp. salt
2 eggs
¼ c. sugar

½ c. dairy sour cream
½ c. melted butter

Gradually add 2¾ to 3 cups flour to form stiff dough. Let rise until double in bulk. Roll dough in *two* 12 inch circles. Brush with melted butter. Combine ¾ cup sugar and ¾ cup coconut; sprinkle over each circle. Cut into 12 wedges. Roll up, starting with wide end. Place in 3 rows in a greased 9x13 inch pan. Let rise. Bake at 350° for 25 to 30 minutes. Leave in pan.

For topping, combine:

¾ c. sugar
½ c. sour cream
¼ c. butter

1 tsp. vanilla
2 Tbsp. orange juice

Boil 3 minutes. Pour glaze over rolls.

Gladys Davis, Iowa

BREAKFAST ROLL

½ c. nuts
1 large loaf frozen bread
1 tsp. cinnamon
1 box instant butterscotch pudding

1 stick margarine
½ c. white sugar
2 Tbsp. brown sugar

493-95

Grease a tube/angel food cake pan. Sprinkle in ½ cup nuts. Slice 1 large or 2 small loaves of frozen bread into ½ inch slices around the pan, overlapping. Sprinkle each slice with cinnamon. Sprinkle ½ box instant butterscotch pudding mix over the bread. Melt 1 stick of margarine with ½ cup white sugar, 2 tablespoons brown sugar, and 1 teaspoon cinnamon. Make a syrup. Pour over the dough. Cover with wax paper and a towel to rise. Bake at 350° for 25 to 30 minutes.

May prepare in the evening, let rise overnight, and bake the next morning.

Lottie Evans, Texas

EASY SWEET ROLLS

1 pkg. white or yellow cake mix
2 eggs
½ tsp. salt

5 or 6 c. flour
2½ c. warm water
2 pkg. yeast

Mix yeast in water and let stand for 10 minutes. Add remaining ingredients. Mix with a spoon. Let stand, covered, for 2 hours. Roll out. Spread with butter, brown sugar, raisins, etc. Roll in a roll. Cut in 1 inch pieces. Place cut pieces in two 9x13 inch greased pans. Let rise until doubled. Bake at 350° for 20 minutes. Frost and serve.

May freeze for later use.

Darlene Ricklefs, Iowa

FAVORITE YEAST ROLLS

1 c. shortening (margarine)
½ c. sugar
1 c. boiling water
1 c. cold water

2 pkg. dry yeast
6 c. unsifted plain flour
1 tsp. salt

Cream shortening and sugar. Slowly add boiling water. When mostly cooled and dissolved, add cold water. When lukewarm, add yeast and dissolve. Add beaten eggs, flour, and salt.

Mix and place in refrigerator overnight. When ready to use, roll out to ½ inch thick. Cut with biscuit cutter. Butter with melted margarine. Fold over and rebutter and place in warm place for 1½ hours. Bake 10 to 12 minutes in 450° oven. Can be frozen. *"Out of this world"* good.

Laura Nelson, Tennessee

FROZEN BREAD ROLLS

2 loaves frozen bread dough
½ c. butter
2 Tbsp. milk
½ tsp. cinnamon

1 large pkg. vanilla pudding (not instant)
1 c. brown sugar

Thaw bread, but do not allow it to rise. Grease a 9x13 inch pan. Cut both loaves into pieces and drop into pan, filling the pan. Melt the butter and add rest of the ingredients. Beat until smooth and pour over the dough. Let rise 2½ to 3 hours. Bake in a 350°F. oven for 30 minutes. Let cool for 10 minutes and turn upside down onto wax paper.

Nellie Value, Iowa

NO KNEAD YEAST ROLLS

4 c. flour
2 packs dry yeast
1 egg
⅓ c. shortening

1 tsp. salt
¼ c. sugar
⅓ c. dry milk
1½ c. lukewarm water

Mix dry ingredients in first bowl. In second bowl, mix warm water and dry yeast. Add dry mixture. Add egg and shortening; mix well, then add 2 cups of flour and mix, then add 2 more cups of flour. Beat until smooth. Let rise 30 minutes, then beat down and form into rolls on baking pan. Let rise 10 or 20 minutes. Bake in a 350° oven for 15 to 20 minutes.

Mrs. Judy Scherer, Missouri

SUNFLOWER SNACK ROLLS

1 pkg. yeast in ¼ c. warm water
1 c. creamed cottage cheese
2 Tbsp. sugar
1 Tbsp. instant minced onion
1 egg
1 Tbsp. Promise sunflower
   margarine

2 tsp. dill seed
1 Tbsp. unsalted sunflower seeds
1 tsp. salt
¼ tsp. soda
2¼ to 2½ c. flour

Mix all ingredients, except flour and yeast, into warmed cottage cheese. Mix well. Add yeast, then add flour. Knead until smooth. Let rise once. Shape into small rolls. Let rise. Bake in a 350° oven about 10 to 12 minutes until golden brown.

Reprinted with permission from the National Sunflower Association.
Esther Olson, North Dakota

WONDERFUL ROLLS

Scald together:

1 qt. milk
1 c. butter Crisco

1 c. sugar

Set aside to cool. Dissolve 1½ tablespoon package yeast in 1 cup warm water. Add to scalded milk when milk has cooled to lukewarm. Peel 3 medium size potatoes, cut into small pieces. Boil until very tender. Drain water and reserve. Mash potatoes. Add 1 cup of reserved water and slowly add milk mixture. Beating with mixer, add enough flour to make a soft dough. Place in large container and let rise until double. Add 1 teaspoon soda, 2 teaspoons baking powder, and 1 teaspoon salt. With mixer, beat until well blended.

Add more flour to make stiff dough, beating with mixer as long as you can, then mix with hands until dough is stiff, but not heavy. Dough will stiffen up after it is put into the refrigerator. Place dough in large container with lid. Refrigerate at least 3 to 4 hours, punching down from time to time, until it stops rising. Can be stored for up to a week in the refrigerator.

Remove dough as you wish to use. Roll out and make into cinnamon rolls or make into small balls for cloverleaf rolls and place in pans. Let rise until double. Bake in 350° oven until done.

Marilyn Cowell, Missouri

ALICE'S DATE NUT BREAD

1 lb. pitted dates (whole or halves)
1 lb. English walnuts (whole or halves)
1 c. flour
4 eggs, separated

1 c. sugar
2 tsp. baking powder
½ tsp. salt
2½ tsp. vanilla

Sift flour, baking powder, and salt together. Add to the dates and nuts. Mix egg yolks, sugar, and vanilla well and add to date mixture. Mix with hands as you would pie dough. Fold in the stiffly beaten egg whites.

Pack into well greased and floured pan. Can use tube pan, loaf pan or two 1 pound coffee cans for this recipe. Press down on all corners. Bake about 1 hour and 15 minutes in a 300° to 325° oven. *Delicious.*

Ruth Kenaley, Iowa

OLD-FASHIONED HOMEMADE BREAD

Have on hand 1 package of beer yeast (available from homemade beer ingredient supplier).

In a bowl, add about 2 quarts of lukewarm potato water. (Water in which potatoes have been boiled or water in which 1 potato has been boiled to a very soft consistency, mashed in the water, and left in the water.) Add about ½ cup of sugar. Let this sit at room temperature overnight or until it becomes very foamy. This should be stirred several times during the period. When ready to use, remove 1 pint of liquid and store this in the refrigerator in a jar with a loose fitting lid for future use. Take the rest of the yeast liquid and add about 3 or 4 tablespoons of vegetable oil, salt (if wanted), sugar (amount can vary according to your wishes - this dough makes excellent sweet rolls) and add all the flour that you can add to make a dough. This dough should not be sticky. It is best to knead as much air into the dough as possible and flour can be added during this process. Allow the dough to double in size and then work it back down. Make the dough into loaves or into rolls. Place in greased pan. Allow to double in size. Bake in a preheated 375° oven until browned. Butter can be brushed on the top. The bread should be removed from the pans immediately and allowed to cool.

The next time you wish to make bread you can use the starter by adding potato water and sugar and letting it stand as before. The yeast starter should be "renewed" as before every 6 to 8 weeks if it is not used. With proper care, it will last for years.

Cliff Smith, Missouri

APRICOT WALNUT BREAD

4 egg whites
½ c. orange juice
1 tsp. vanilla
⅔ c. water
¼ c. vegetable oil
¾ c. uncooked oat bran hot cereal

½ c. chopped dried apricots
1¼ c. all-purpose flour
½ c. packed brown sugar
1 tsp. baking powder
½ tsp. baking soda
¼ c. chopped walnuts

In a bowl, combine the first 5 ingredients. Stir in oat bran and apricots. Combine flour, brown sugar, baking powder, and soda; stir into apricot mixture just until moistened. Fold in nuts. Pour into a greased 8x4x2 inch loaf pan. Bake at 350° for 50 to 55 minutes or until bread tests done. Cool in pan 10 minutes. Remove to wire rack. Yields 1 loaf.

Diabetic exchanges: 1 slice equals 1 starch, 1 fat, ½ fruit. Also, 141 calories, 42 mg sodium, 0 cholesterol, 20 grams carbohydrate, and 4 grams protein.

Johanna Kruse, Minnesota

OATMEAL MAPLE-RAISIN BREAD

2 pkg. active dry yeast
½ c. warm water
1½ c. boiling water
1 c. raisins
1 c. quick-cooking oatmeal

½ c. maple blended syrup
2 tsp. salt
1 Tbsp. shortening
4½ to 5 c. flour

Soften yeast in ½ cup warm water. Pour boiling water over raisins and oatmeal; cool to lukewarm. Add maple syrup, salt, shortening, and yeast to raisins and oats. Beat in about 4½ cups flour. Turn onto lightly floured board and knead 8 to 10 minutes, or until smooth and elastic. Place in lightly greased bowl. Turn once to grease surface and let rise in warm place until double in bulk, about 1 hour. Punch down; divide into 2 portions. Let rest 10 minutes. Shape into 2 loaves and place into 2 greased 8½ x 4½ x 2½ inch loaf pans. Bake in 375° oven for 40 minutes. Cool on rack.

Judith Materna, North Dakota

BANANA BREAD

¾ c. shortening
1½ c. sugar
3 eggs
1½ c. ripe banana pulp
3 c. flour

2¼ tsp. baking powder
¾ tsp. soda
1 tsp. salt
4½ tsp. milk
1½ tsp. lemon juice

Preheat oven to 350°. Grease 4 small or 2 regular size loaf pans. Cream ¾ cup shortening and 1½ cups sugar. Beat in 3 beaten eggs and 1½ cups ripe banana pulp. In a separate bowl, sift together 3 cups flour, 2¼ teaspoons baking powder, ¾ teaspoon soda, and 1 teaspoon salt. Beat in with the preceding mixture in 3 parts. Beat until smooth after each addition. Add 4½ teaspoons milk and 1½ teaspoons lemon juice. Mix well. Add 1½ cups nuts. Bake 55 minutes.

Mark and Cathy Perrin, AgriTalk

BEER BREAD

3 c. self-rising flour
1 can regular beef (at room
    temperature)

3 Tbsp. sugar
1 egg

Stir ingredients together and pour into a greased loaf pan. Bake in a 375° oven for 30 minutes.

So simple and delicious - plus easy!

Marilyn Miller, Colorado

COLONIAL BREAD

Combine:

1/2 c. corn meal
1/2 c. brown sugar or 1/3 c. honey

1/2 c. vegetable oil

Pour 2 cups boiling potato water over preceding. Let cool until lukewarm. Add 1 tablespoon dry yeast which has been dissolved in 1/2 cup warm water.

Add:

3/4 c. whole wheat flour

1/2 c. rye flour

Add 4 1/2 to 5 1/2 cups white flour. Knead until stiff. Let rise until double in bulk. Work down and let rise again, then put in individual loaf pans. Let rise and bake at 350° for 40 to 45 minutes.

Doris McElroy, Illinois

CORN BREAD

1 "Jiffy" corn bread muffin mix

1 "Jiffy" yellow cake mix

Mix both packages as each are directed in one bowl. Bake as directed on box in a 9x9 inch pan. Serve warm with butter and honey.

ENGLISH MUFFIN BATTER BREAD

1 c. warm water (105° to 110°)
2 pkg. yeast
2 Tbsp. sugar
Scant salt
About 5 c. flour

1 1/2 c. warm milk
1/2 tsp. baking soda, dissolved in 1
    Tbsp. water
Corn meal for dusting

Combine water, yeast, and sugar. Let stand 15 minutes until bubbly. Grease the inside of three 1 pound coffee cans and dust thoroughly with corn meal.

With electric mixer, beat salt, 3 cups flour, and 1 cup milk into yeast mixture. Add these ingredients alternately and beat well after each addition.

Add soda water mixture and beat well. With spoon, beat in remaining milk and enough flour to make a heavy dough that's too sticky to knead. Spoon dough equally into cans and top with greased coffee can lids or waxed paper. Let rise until lids pop off, about 45 to 60 minutes. Carefully remove lids and bake bread in a 350° oven for 25 to 30 minutes. Slide out and let stand upright to cool.

Mary Ann Olson, South Dakota

MEXICAN CORN BREAD

1 c. corn meal
¾ c. milk
1 egg, beaten
2 Tbsp. vegetable oil
1½ tsp. sugar
1 tsp. baking powder
½ c. canned cream style corn

¼ c. chopped onion
1½ tsp. seeded jalapeno peppers, chopped
3 slices bacon, cooked crisp and crumbled
¾ c. shredded Cheddar cheese

Grease an 8 inch cast iron skillet with 1 tablespoon oil. Combine all ingredients in bowl and stir well. Heat skillet in 425° oven for 10 minutes. Pour batter into hot skillet. Bake at 425° for 20 minutes or until golden brown.

Sue Clearman, Texas

ONION SPIRAL BREAD

2 Tbsp. granulated yeast
3 Tbsp. plus 1 tsp. sugar
2½ c. warm water
1 Tbsp. salt

3 eggs, slightly beaten
¼ c. vegetable oil
8½ to 9 c. all-purpose flour

Filling:

¼ c. butter
4 c. diced onion
2 garlic cloves, minced
½ tsp. dried thyme
½ tsp. basil

½ tsp. oregano
2 c. grated Swiss cheese
1 c. grated Parmesan cheese
½ c. minced fresh parsley
Salt and pepper

In a small bowl, combine the yeast, 1 teaspoon sugar, and ¼ cup water. Set aside 5 minutes. In a large bowl, combine the remaining 2 cups water, 1 tablespoon salt, the 3 beaten eggs, the ¼ cup oil, and remaining 3 tablespoons sugar. Stir in the yeast mixture. Beat in flour, 1 cup at a time, to form a stiff dough. Knead for 10 minutes. Turn into a greased bowl.

Meanwhile, melt the butter in a saute pan and saute the onions, garlic, and herbs, except parsley. Saute until limp, 3 to 5 minutes.

Transfer to a bowl and cool to room temperature, then add parsley and Swiss and Parmesan cheeses. Season to taste with salt and pepper. Punch down bread dough. Divide in half. Roll out each half into a 9x12 inch rectangle and spread half the onion-cheese mixture on each rectangle. Roll up in jelly roll fashion. Place on baking sheet and brush with egg white and 2 tablespoons sesame seed. Bake at 350° for 45 minutes.

Lydia Stelting, Kansas

STRAWBERRY BREAD

3 c. flour
2 c. sugar
1 tsp. salt
1 tsp. baking soda
1 tsp. cinnamon

4 eggs
1½ c. oil
1 c. chopped pecans
1 (16 oz.) bag frozen strawberries,
    thawed

In a bowl, sift together all dry ingredients. In a large bowl, beat eggs and oil. Add pecans and strawberries. When well blended, start to add the dry mixture with the wet (a little at a time). Pour 1 cup of the batter into well greased and floured mini loaf pans. Bake 1 hour (or until done) at 350°. Makes 5 to 7 mini loaves.

This bread freezes well and will keep up to 1 month if well wrapped and bagged.

Nancy L. McGovern, Missouri

SUGAR 'N SPICE BREAD

2 pkg. dry yeast
½ c. warm water
½ c. butter
⅓ c. sugar
2 tsp. salt

1 c. hot scalded milk
1 unbeaten egg
4 to 4½ c. flour (approx.)
½ c. Malt-O Meal

Soften yeast in water. Combine butter, sugar, salt, and scalded milk; cool to lukewarm. Blend 1 egg and yeast. Add 2 cups of flour and Malt-O Meal. Beat until smooth. Add remaining flour gradually to form a stiff dough, beating well after each addition. Cover. Let rise in warm place until doubled, about 1½ hours. Divide dough into 2 balls. Roll each into 7x12 inch rectangle on lightly floured board. Brush dough with slightly beaten egg white. Sprinkle with mixture of ½ cup sugar and 1 tablespoon cinnamon. Roll short end toward you, jelly roll fashion. Seal well. Place in greased pans, filling no more than half full. Cover. Let rise in warm place until doubled, about 30 minutes. Bake 35 to 40 minutes in preheated oven at 375°. Makes 2 loaves.

This is great bread. Try it. Tasty.

Irene Heuer, North Dakota

ZUCCHINI BREAD

3 eggs
2 c. sugar
1 c. oil
3 c. flour
1 tsp. salt
1 tsp. soda

1 tsp. baking powder
1 tsp. cinnamon
1½ tsp. vanilla
¾ c. nuts, chopped
2 c. grated zucchini squash

Beat eggs and sugar until thick and lemon colored. Add oil. Add flour, salt, soda, baking powder, and cinnamon. Add vanilla. Stir well. Fold in nuts and zucchini. Pour mixture into 2 well greased and floured loaf pans. Bake at 350° for 1 hour.

Rebecca Norris, Minnesota

NO KNEAD SWEET DOUGH

2 pkg. yeast
2 c. warm water
1 Tbsp. salt
½ c. sugar

2 c. flour
2 eggs
⅓ c. melted shortening
4½ c. flour

Mix together ingredients. Set aside 30 minutes. Form into desired shapes, then let rise for 1 hour. Bake at 350° for 20 minutes.

I use this recipe for cinnamon rolls and is very good.

Connie Schaefers, Iowa

NUTRITIOUS SUNFLOWER AND WHOLE WHEAT MUFFINS

1 c. flour
2½ tsp. baking powder
¼ tsp. salt (optional)
1 c. whole wheat flour
½ c. roasted sunflower seeds
  (salted or unsalted)

½ c. raisins
1 egg
¾ c. milk
⅓ c. sunflower oil
⅓ c. honey

Stir flour, baking powder, and salt. Add whole wheat flour, sunflower seeds, and raisins. Stir well. Beat egg, milk, oil, and honey together and add all at once to dry ingredients. Stir just until moistened. Fill greased or paper lined muffin cups ⅔ full. Bake in a 400° oven for 20 to 25 minutes. Makes 1 dozen muffins.

Reprinted with permission from the National Sunflower Association.

Cherie Olson, North Dakota

PECAN STICKY BUNS

3 Tbsp. margarine
½ c. chopped pecans
⅓ c. brown sugar

¼ c. coconut
½ tsp. cinnamon
1 pkg. refrigerated biscuits

Preheat oven to 375°. Melt 3 tablespoons of margarine. Stir in ½ cup chopped pecans, ⅓ cup brown sugar, ¼ cup coconut, and ½ teaspoon cinnamon. Spread evenly in a 9x9 inch pan. Arrange refrigerated biscuits on top. Bake 20 minutes or until golden. Cool in pan 1 minute. Invert onto plate.

Dorothy Evans, Texas

RAISED DONUTS

1 pkg. yeast
¼ c. warm water
1 c. scalded milk, cooled
¼ c. shortening
¼ c. sugar

½ tsp. salt
¾ c. mashed potatoes
2 eggs
5 to 6 c. flour

Dissolve yeast in warm water. Combine milk, shortening, sugar, and salt. Stir in eggs, yeast, and potatoes. Gradually add flour to make a smooth dough. Turn out onto floured surface and knead until satiny. Let rise until double. Roll out dough to ½ inch thickness. Cut with doughnut cutter. Let rise 30 minutes.

493-95

Fry in oil at 375°. Turn only once. While still slightly warm, dip in glaze. I use my electric fry pan to fry in.

Glaze:

1 lb. powdered sugar
6 Tbsp. warm water

1 tsp. vanilla

Mix well.

Peg Fast, South Dakota

RHUBARB MUFFINS

1¼ c. brown sugar
½ c. cooking oil
1 egg
2 tsp. vanilla
1 c. buttermilk
1½ c. diced rhubarb
½ c. chopped walnuts

¼ tsp. black walnut or almond
    flavoring
2½ c. flour
1 tsp. soda
1 tsp. baking powder
½ tsp. salt

In large bowl, combine brown sugar, oil, egg, vanilla, and buttermilk; mix well. Stir in rhubarb, walnuts, and flavoring. In sifter, combine flour, soda, baking powder, and salt. Add to rhubarb mixture. Spoon batter into muffin pans.

Topping:

1 tsp. melted butter or margarine
1 tsp. cinnamon

⅓ c. sugar

Spoon onto muffins and press down. Bake about 20 minutes at 350°. Makes 18 muffins.

Eileen Baird, Minnesota

SUNNY RING

1 pkg. active dry yeast
¼ c. warm water (110°F.)
⅓ c. milk
¼ c. granulated sugar
3 Tbsp. sunflower margarine
½ tsp. salt

2 eggs
¼ c. sunflower kernel, roasted,
    salted and finely ground
2 to 2½ c. bread flour
½ tsp. baking soda

Filling:

½ c. sunflower kernel, roasted and
    chopped

½ c. melted sunflower margarine
½ c. brown sugar

Dissolve yeast in ¼ cup warm water. Let stand. Warm milk and pour over sugar, margarine, and salt in mixing bowl. Beat eggs and add to preceding mixture. Stir in ½ cup flour and the ground sunflower kernel. Cool to lukewarm. Add yeast. Add enough flour to make a soft, manageable dough. Cover and let rest 8 to 10 minutes. Knead 10 minutes or until blisters can be seen. Put dough in a greased bowl. Grease surface of dough. Let rise until doubled. Punch down.

Roll into a 9x24 inch rectangle. Pour ½ cup melted margarine over dough. Spread within 1 inch of all sides. Sprinkle with sunflower kernel and brown sugar.

Roll jelly roll fashion. Pinch edges together firmly. Connect ends to make a circle and place on a well greased cookie sheet or pizza pan. With scissors, cut from outside in every 1½ inches, making sure not to cut all the way through. Turn cut edges up. Let rise until doubled. Bake in a preheated 375°F. oven for about 20 minutes. Cool 5 minutes and invert pan to remove Sunny Ring.

Reprinted with permission from the National Sunflower Association.

Judi Hornseth, North Dakota

Notes

Desserts

HANDY CHART OF KITCHEN MATH
(Size of Pans and Baking Dishes)

Cooking need never become a crisis, when you use our handy charts. Need a 4 or 6-cup baking dish? Will your fancy mold be the right size for the recipe? See below for the answers.

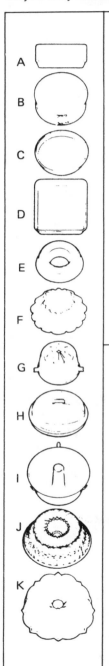

COMMON KITCHEN PANS TO USE AS CASSEROLES WHEN THE RECIPE CALLS FOR:

4-cup baking dish:
9-inch pie plate
8x1¼-inch layer cake pan - **C**
7⅜x3⅝x2¼-inch loaf pan - **A**

6-cup baking dish:
8 or 9x1½-inch layer cake pan - **C**
10-inch pie plate
8½x3⅝x2⅝-inch loaf pan - **A**

8-cup baking dish:
8x8x2-inch square pan - **D**
11x7x1½-inch baking pan
9x5x3-inch loaf pan - **A**

10-cup baking dish:
9x9x2-inch square pan - **D**
11¾x7½x1¾-inch baking pan
15x10x1-inch jelly-roll pan

12-cup baking dish and over:

13½x8½x2-inch glass baking pan	12 cups
13x9x2-inch metal baking pan	15 cups
14x10½x2½-inch roasting pan	19 cups

TOTAL VOLUME OF VARIOUS SPECIAL BAKING PANS

Tube Pans:

7½x3-inch "Bundt" tube pan - **K**	6 cups
9x3½-inch fancy tube or "Bundt" pan - **J** or **K**	9 cups
9x3½-inch angel cake pan - **I**	12 cups
10x3¾-inch "Bundt" or "Crownburst" pan - **K**	12 cups
9x3½-inch fancy tube mold - **J**	12 cups
10x4-inch fancy tube mold (Kugelhupf) - **J**	16 cups
10x4-inch angel cake pan - **I**	18 cups

Melon Mold:

7x5½x4-inch mold - **H**	6 cups

Spring-Form Pans:

8x3-inch pan - **B**	12 cups
9x3-inch pan - **B**	16 cups

Ring Molds:

8½x2¼-inch mold - **E**	4½ cups
9¼x2¾-inch mold - **E**	8 cups

Charlotte Mold:

6x4¼-inch mold - **G**	7½ cups

Brioche Pan:

9½x3¼-inch pan - **F**	8 cups

DESSERTS

TEXAS CHOCOLATE SHEET CAKE

1¼ c. margarine
½ c. baking cocoa
1 c. water
1½ c. firmly packed brown sugar
2 c. unsifted flour
1 tsp. cinnamon
½ tsp. salt

1 tsp. baking soda
1 (14 oz.) Eagle Brand condensed
   milk
2 eggs
1 tsp. vanilla
1 c. sifted confectioners sugar
1 c. chopped nuts

Heat oven to 350°F. In a small saucepan, melt 1 cup margarine. Stir in ¼ cup baking cocoa, then water. Bring to a boil and remove from heat. In a large bowl, combine flour, brown sugar, baking soda, cinnamon, and salt. Add cocoa mixture; beat well. Stir in ⅓ cup condensed milk, eggs, and vanilla. Pour into greased 15x10 inch jellyroll pan. Bake 15 minutes or until cake springs back when touched.

In a small saucepan, melt remaining ¼ cup margarine. Add ¼ cup baking cocoa and condensed milk. Stir in sifted confectioners sugar and nuts. Spread on warm cake.

Etta Winter, New York

SOUR CREAM COFFEE CAKE

1 c. butter (at room temperature -
   1½ sticks for microwave)
3 c. sugar
6 eggs (at room temperature)
¼ tsp. salt

¼ tsp. soda
3 c. flour
1 scant c. sour cream
1 tsp. vanilla extract

Topping:

2 c. chopped pecans
8 Tbsp. dark brown sugar

4 tsp. ground cinnamon

Cream butter and sugar. Add eggs, one at a time, beating well after each addition. Sift salt, soda, and flour together 3 times. Alternately add sour cream and flour mixture, ending with flour mixture. Add vanilla. Grease a tube pan.

Mix topping ingredients and sprinkle a small amount on the bottom of the pan. Add ½ batter. Sprinkle on more topping. Bake at 300° for 1½ hours. Do not open oven door for the first hour of baking. Makes 8 to 10 servings. Double for larger cake.

For microwave: Cool on level 3 Combo 25 to 30 minutes.

Marilyn Cowell, Missouri

CUPCAKES THAT FILL THEMSELVES

1 pkg. chocolate cake mix
1 (8 oz.) cream cheese
⅓ c. sugar

Dash of salt
1 egg
1 c. chocolate chips

Prepare cake as directed and fill 30 paper cups in muffin tins ⅔ full. Cream together cream cheese, sugar, salt, and egg. Stir in chocolate chips. Drop by teaspoon into each cupcake. Bake at 350° for 20 to 25 minutes or until done.

Robin Miedema, North Dakota

MOTHER'S COFFEE CAKE

¼ c. soft margarine	1½ c. flour
¾ c. sugar	2 tsp. baking powder
1 egg	½ tsp. salt
½ c. milk	

1. Cream margarine and sugar; add egg and blend well. Stir in milk.
2. Sift together flour, baking powder, and salt. Add to batter; set aside.

Topping:

3 Tbsp. melted margarine	2 tsp. cinnamon
¾ c. brown sugar	½ c. chopped nuts

1. Mix ingredients together.
2. In a greased 9x9 inch pan, spread ½ the batter and sprinkle with ½ the topping. Repeat.
2. Bake at 375° for 25 to 30 minutes.

This yummy treat uses ingredients found in every kitchen. It smells wonderful while it's baking, too.

Miriam Hanson, Iowa

MOIST CHOCOLATE CAKE

1 c. oil (prefer Crisco)	2 eggs
1 c. sour milk or buttermilk (prefer buttermilk)	

Beat together the preceding 3 ingredients.

Measure before sifting:

2 c. white sugar	1 tsp. (heaping) baking soda
2 c. flour	¼ tsp. salt
½ c. cocoa (prefer Hershey's)	

Sift together the 5 dry ingredients. Add this to the first mixture. Mix well, then add 1 cup boiling hot water and 2 teaspoons vanilla. Mix well. Pour into a 9x13 inch cake pan. Bake in a 300° oven for 1 hour. Cool.

Good without frosting or frost with your favorite frosting.

Orlene Renner Schaper, North Dakota

IOWA CHOCOLATE CAKE

¾ c. shortening
2 c. sugar
1½ c. boiling water
2 c. flour
2 tsp. baking soda

½ c. cocoa
½ tsp. salt
2 eggs, beaten
1 tsp. vanilla

Place shortening and sugar in bowl. Cover with boiling water and mix. Sift dry ingredients and add to hot mixture. Mix well. Lastly, add eggs and vanilla. Mix again. Batter will be very thin. Pour into greased and floured 9x13 inch pan. Bake at 350°F. for 25 to 35 minutes.

This is an excellent chocolate cake! The recipe is one my mother had.

Jean Boyer, Iowa

CHOCOLATE CHEESECAKE

1 pkg. chocolate cake mix
2 Tbsp. oil
2 pkg. (8 oz.) cream cheese,
    softened

½ c. sugar
4 eggs
1½ c. milk
1 tsp. vanilla

Preheat oven to 300°. Reserve 1 cup of dry cake mix. In large bowl, mix remaining cake mix, 1 egg, and oil. Mixture will be crumbly. Press on bottom of greased 9x13 inch pan. In second bowl, blend cream cheese and sugar; add 3 eggs and reserved cake mix. Beat 1 minute at medium speed. At low speed, slowly add milk and vanilla; mix until smooth. Pour over crust. Bake 45 to 55 minutes until center is firm. Top with Cool Whip.

Mary Santel, Illinois

ROYAL APPLE CAKE

2 c. diced apples (or canned apples
    plus sugar)

1 c. sugar

Let stand about 30 minutes or until juice is just right.

1 c. flour
1 egg, beaten
¼ c. Mazola oil
1 tsp. soda

1 tsp. cinnamon
1 tsp. salt
1 tsp. vanilla
½ c. nuts

Sift dry ingredients. Mix everything. Bake at 300° for 15 minutes, then at 350° for 15 minutes. Test if done. Put in an 8x8 inch pan. If you double recipe, put in a 9x13 inch pan.

Topping:

1 c. sugar
1 Tbsp. cornstarch
½ c. margarine

1 c. water
1 tsp. vanilla

Cook until thick. Pour over warm cake. Top with Cool Whip and cherry. Serve and enjoy. I usually wait and put topping on when I am ready to serve.

Betty Seidt, Missouri

MOON CAKE

1 stick margarine   1 c. water

Bring to a boil. Add 1 cup flour. Stir until it sticks together. Add 4 eggs, one at a time, and beat vigorously with a wire whip. Pat into a 10x15 inch pan. (Wet fingers to keep dough from sticking to fingers.) Bake at 350° for 20 to 25 minutes or until golden brown. (Will rise like a cream puff.)

Mix:

2 pkg. butter pecan instant pudding   8 oz. softened cream cheese
3½ c. milk

Mix together until thick. Pour over baked crust. Spread Cool Whip over the top (8 or 12 ounces) of the pudding mixture. Drizzle chocolate syrup over the Cool Whip and top with cherries.

Rayma Fiegen, North Dakota

SWEEPSTAKES COFFEE CAKE

½ c. oleo or butter   2 c. flour
1 c. sugar   1 tsp. soda
2 eggs   1 tsp. baking powder
1 Tbsp. vanilla   1 c. sour cream

Topping:

⅓ c. brown sugar   ½ tsp. cinnamon
¼ c. white sugar   1 c. nuts, chopped

Cream oleo and sugar; add eggs, one at a time, and mix. Stir in vanilla and dry ingredients which have been sifted together. Add sour cream and mix.

Combine topping ingredients. Put ½ of batter in a 9x13 inch pan that has been greased and floured. Sprinkle ½ of topping over batter. Add rest of batter, then add rest of topping. Bake 40 minutes in a 350° oven. Serves 12 or 15.

Norma Schaaf, Iowa

APPLE CAKE

3 c. flour   2 eggs, beaten
1½ c. sugar   1 c. oil
1 tsp. soda   3 c. apples, chopped
1 tsp. cinnamon   1 c. nuts, chopped

Sift together the first 4 ingredients. Add eggs and oil to the dry mix and stir, then add the apples and nuts. Mix well. Spread in 9x13 inch greased pan. Sprinkle with brown sugar and bake at 350° for 40 to 45 minutes until toothpick comes out dry. Serve with Cool Whip or sauce.

Bernadene Carlson, Illinois

STRAWBERRY CAKE

Beat all for 4 minutes:

1 box white cake mix
1 small pkg. strawberry jello
½ c. oil
**½ c. drained frozen strawberries (or
    fresh)**

½ c. water
4 eggs

Spread in a 9x12 inch greased and floured pan and bake at 350° for 35 to 40 minutes.

Frosting:

½ c. soft oleo
½ c. strawberries

1 lb. powdered sugar

Mix and spread on cooled cake.

Anna Marie Hamlink, Illinois

OATMEAL CAKE

1¼ c. boiling water   **1 c. oatmeal**

Pour water over oatmeal and let set while you mix the rest.

Cream:

½ c. butter or margarine
1 c. brown sugar

1 c. white sugar

Add:

2 eggs
¼ tsp. salt

1 tsp. vanilla

Add oatmeal mixture alternately with:

1½ c. flour
1 tsp. cinnamon

1 tsp. soda

Bake at 350° for 35 minutes.

Topping:

5 Tbsp. brown sugar
3 Tbsp. butter

2 Tbsp. milk

Bring to a boil and remove from heat. Add powdered sugar and coconut if desired. Beat to spreading consistency.

Maxine Christensen, Iowa

APPLE COFFEE CAKE

1 c. butter	1 c. flour
1 c. sugar	1/2 tsp. baking powder
1 c. sour cream	1/2 tsp. soda
1 large egg	1 tsp. vanilla

Mix well. Mix 4 cups sliced apples and 1 (3 ounce) strawberry jello.

Top with:

1 c. flour	1/2 c. butter
1 c. sugar	

Mix well and put on top of cake. Put in a greased 9x13 inch pan and bake at 350° for 45 minutes.

Shirley Hummel, Wisconsin

FOOLPROOF CHOCOLATE CAKE

2 c. sugar	2 1/2 c. flour
1/2 c. butter	1 tsp. vanilla
2 eggs	1/4 c. cocoa
1 c. buttermilk	

Put the cocoa and 1 teaspoon soda in a bowl and pour over it 1/2 cup boiling water. Let this stand while the remainder of the cake is mixed. This step is important so be sure to follow it correctly.

Mix the rest of the cake by creaming the sugar and butter; add the eggs, then the flour and buttermilk alternately. Add the vanilla and the cocoa mixture last. Pour into a greased and floured 9x13 inch pan. Bake in a 350° oven for 45 minutes.

Broiled Icing for the cake:

6 Tbsp. melted butter	4 Tbsp. cream
10 Tbsp. brown sugar	1 c. flaked coconut

Mix and place on cake while it is still warm. Place under the broiler with the flame turned low. Broil until it bubbles on the surface.

Mrs. Marvin Kirby, Missouri

MOIST CHOCOLATE CAKE

2 c. all-purpose flour	1 c. vegetable oil
1 tsp. salt	1 c. hot coffee
1 tsp. baking powder	1 c. milk
2 tsp. baking soda	2 eggs
1/2 c. unsweetened cocoa	1 tsp. vanilla extract
2 c. sugar	

Sift dry ingredients in a mixing bowl. Add oil, coffee, and milk; mix at medium speed 2 minutes. Add eggs and vanilla; beat 2 more minutes. (Batter will be thin.) Pour into 2 greased and floured 9 x 1 1/2 inch cake pans (or two 8 inch cake pans and six muffin cups). Bake at 325° for 25 to 30 minutes. Cool cakes before removing from pans.

This cake is excellent for birthday cakes for the grandchildren.

Karen Hintz, Nebraska

FRESH APPLE CAKE

2 eggs
2 c. white sugar
1 tsp. cinnamon
1 tsp. soda
1 c. coconut

1 c. cooking oil
3 c. flour
1 tsp. salt
3 c. fresh apples, diced
1 c. chopped pecans

Mix together eggs, oil, and sugar. Add dry ingredients, then apples and nuts. Bake at 350° about 1 hour to 1 hour and 15 minutes in a 9x13 inch pan. Pour on icing while hot.

Icing:

1 c. powdered sugar   Juice of 1 lemon

Mix together and pour over cake while hot.

Rebecca Kirk, Missouri

FRUIT COCKTAIL CAKE

2 c. sugar
2 c. flour
2 eggs
1 (No. 303) can fruit cocktail

2 tsp. soda
1 tsp. baking powder
1 tsp. salt

Sift together flour, sugar, soda, baking powder, and salt. Add eggs and fruit cocktail (liquid also). Mix all together with a mixer for 10 minutes. Bake at 350° for 35 to 40 minutes in a buttered loaf pan.

Easy Icing:

1 c. sugar
1 stick oleo

1 small can Pet milk

Cook, stirring until thick, and add ½ cup coconut.

Deloris Orton, Missouri

EASY COFFEE CAKE

1 box yellow cake mix
2 eggs
1 can Thank You vanilla pudding
½ c. sugar

½ c. nuts
6 oz. butterscotch bits or ½ cup
    butter brickle bits

Mix first 3 ingredients together and spread in a 9x13 inch cake pan. Mix sugar, nuts, and bits together; spread over cake and swirl through cake with a knife. Bake at 350° for 25 to 30 minutes.

Ruthina Forgey, Indiana

493-95

HAWAII SPLENDOR SPONGE CAKE

2 c. flour
1½ c. sugar
1 tsp. baking soda

2 eggs
¼ tsp. salt
1 (20 oz.) can crushed pineapple

Mix together. Pour in a lightly floured 9x13 inch pan. Bake at 350° for 30 minutes. Cool 10 minutes in pan. Spread Golden Frosting on warm cake.

Golden Frosting - In a saucepan, combine:

¾ c. sugar
¾ c. evaporated milk

½ c. butter
1 tsp. vanilla

Bring to a boil. Boil 10 to 12 minutes, stirring constantly until thick. Stir in ½ cup chopped nuts and ½ cup flaked coconut.

Mary Ann Olson, South Dakota

APRICOT KUCHEN (COFFEE CAKE)

Pillsbury hot roll mix
2 c. whipping cream
½ c. sugar

4 Tbsp. flour
1 large can or 2 small cans apricots

Grease a jelly roll pan; mix hot roll mix as directed. In small saucepan, heat 2 cups whipping cream, ½ cup sugar, and 4 tablespoons flour. Spread ½ of cooked mixture when cool over roll mix that's been spread in jelly roll pan. Drain apricots and put over creamy layer. Top with remaining creamy mixture and sprinkle with cinnamon. Bake at 325° until lightly browned and dough is done.

Susan Conner, Iowa

CHOCOLATE CHIP ZUCCHINI CAKE

Cream:

1¾ c. sugar
½ c. vegetable oil

½ c. soft shortening

Add:

2 eggs
½ tsp. vanilla

½ c. sour cream or milk

Add:

2½ c. flour
½ tsp. baking powder
½ tsp. cloves

4 Tbsp. cocoa
1 tsp. baking soda
½ tsp. cinnamon

Add 2 cups grated deseeded zucchini. Sprinkle ½ cup chocolate chips over the top. Bake in a 13x9x2 inch pan for 40 to 45 minutes at 350°. Dust with confectioners sugar.

Must be kept in refrigerator. Will mold in hot weather very quickly. Can't tell mold from confectioners sugar.

Nancy Matlock, Indiana

JELLY ROLL CAKE

1 c. sugar
1 c. flour
1 tsp. cream of tartar

3 eggs
3 Tbsp. milk
½ tsp. soda

Mix sugar and eggs. Add rest of ingredients. Bake at 350° for 12 to 15 minutes in well greased jelly roll pan. Turn out on towel. Spread with jelly and roll out.

Marie Denner, Iowa

CREAM CHEESE POUND CAKE

1½ c. (3 sticks) butter
1 (8 oz.) pkg. cream cheese
3 c. sugar
6 eggs

1½ tsp. vanilla
3 c. flour
¼ tsp. salt

Preheat oven to 325°. Grease and flour a 10 inch tube pan or 12 cup Bundt pan. Beat butter and cream cheese together in a mixing bowl until well blended. Add sugar to mixture and cream until light and fluffy. Add eggs, one at a time. Blend in vanilla. Blend flour and salt into creamed mixture. Spoon batter into prepared pan. Bake 1 hour and 15 minutes or until toothpick comes out clean. Cool in pan 5 minutes. Turn out on wire rack. Dust with confectioners sugar. Makes 12 to 15 servings.

Violet Ward, Florida

PUNCH BOWL CAKE

1 box yellow cake mix
2 small pkg. noninstant vanilla
pudding mix
2 boxes frozen drained strawberries
(save juice)
5 bananas, sliced and sprinkled
with lemon juice

1 large can drained sweet light
pineapple (crushed)
1 large ctn. Cool Whip
Cherries

Bake cake. Cool and crumble in a big see-through bowl. Cook pudding and set aside to cool. Put strawberries over cake. Pour 1 cup of juice from strawberries over the cake. Add bananas and crushed pineapple. Add a layer of cooled pudding. Add a layer of Cool Whip. Add cherries on top.

Brenda Watkins, Texas

FRUIT COCKTAIL CAKE

2½ c. flour
2 c. sugar
2 tsp. soda
½ tsp. salt

2 eggs
1 large can fruit cocktail
2 tsp. vanilla

Mix dry ingredients. Add eggs, vanilla, and fruit cocktail.

Top with:

1½ c. brown sugar

½ c. nutmeats

Bake at 350° for 30 to 40 minutes.

Mrs. Aileen P. Anderson, Wisconsin

APPLESAUCE CAKE

1½ c. sugar
½ c. shortening
2 eggs
1½ c. thick applesauce
1 c. raisins, cooked
½ c. hot raisin juice
2 tsp. soda

1 tsp. cinnamon
1 tsp. allspice
½ tsp. cloves
½ tsp. salt
2½ c. flour
½ c. nuts

Cover 1 cup raisins with water. Bring to a boil. Cool. Add enough water with raisin juice to make ½ cup. Cream together shortening and sugar. Add eggs and mix very well. Add soda, salt, cinnamon, allspice, and cloves. Mix. Add applesauce, ½ cup liquid, and nuts. Stir well. Add the flour and drained raisins with a spoon until well mixed.

Pour in a greased 9x13 inch cake pan. Bake at 350° for 45 minutes. Dust top of cake with powdered sugar if desired.

Mary Berger, South Dakota

MATRIMONY CAKE

1 tsp. vanilla
1 c. butter or margarine
1 tsp. soda in flour
1½ c. flour

1½ c. brown sugar
2 c. oatmeal (old-fashioned)
½ tsp. salt

Filling - Let boil until thick:

1 c. water
1 c. raisins
2 Tbsp. flour

1 tsp. vanilla
½ c. white sugar

Use low oven (350°). Put ½ of the top recipe in the bottom of a 9x9 inch pan, then put the filling on top of that and sprinkle the other ½ of top recipe on top. Bake for ½ hour in oven.

This recipe has no eggs in it, which makes it unique.

Debra Nachtigall, South Dakota

GOLDEN CRUNCHY COFFEE CAKE

3 c. flour, sifted
3 tsp. baking powder
½ tsp. salt
1½ c. white sugar
½ c. butter

1 tsp. vanilla
4 eggs
1 c. milk
1 c. walnuts, chopped

Mixture:

1 c. brown sugar, firmly packed
2 Tbsp. flour

2 Tbsp. butter
1 tsp. cinnamon

Sift together dry ingredients. Cream together ½ cup butter and sugar until light and fluffy. Add vanilla and eggs, beating well. Add dry ingredients alternately with milk, blending well after each addition. Spread half the batter in greased 13x9x2 inch baking pan.

Combine remaining ingredients. Sprinkle ½ of mixture over batter. Spread with remaining batter; top with remaining crumbs. Bake in a 350° oven for 45 minutes or until done.

Dorothy Carey, Illinois

POOR MAN'S CAKE

2 c. sugar
2 c. cold coffee
2 c. raisins
2 sticks oleo

1 tsp. cinnamon
1 tsp. nutmeg
½ tsp. cloves
2 tsp. soda

Put in pan and heat until oleo is melted. Remove from heat.

Add with mixer:

3 c. flour
½ tsp. baking powder

Nuts

Bake in greased 9x13 inch pan at 350° for 45 minutes. Serve plain or glaze.
Shirley Townsend, Iowa

KELLI'S PRIZE-WINNING CHOCOLATE SHEET CAKE

2 c. sugar
2 c. all-purpose flour
½ c. butter
¼ c. baking cocoa
½ c. oil
1 c. water

2 eggs, beaten
½ c. buttermilk
1 tsp. vanilla
1 tsp. soda
¼ tsp. salt

Mix sugar and flour in mixer bowl. Bring butter, oil, cocoa, and water to a boil in saucepan. Pour over sugar/flour mixture; mix well. Beat in eggs. Add buttermilk, soda, salt, and vanilla, mixing well. Spoon batter into a greased and floured sheet cake or jelly roll pan. Bake at 350° for 25 to 30 minutes. While baking, prepare frosting (following) as you will frost the cake while still warm.

Sheet Cake Icing:

6 Tbsp. milk
½ c. butter
¼ c. baking cocoa

1 lb. powdered sugar
1 tsp. vanilla
1 c. chopped pecans (optional)

Bring milk, butter, and cocoa to a boil in saucepan. Add powdered sugar and vanilla. Beat until smooth and creamy. Spread over warm cake; sprinkle pecans over icing.

Daunita Cordes, Missouri

493-95

CHOCOLATE SAUCE CAKE

Sauce:

2 c. sugar
4 Tbsp. butter
3 c. water

2 Tbsp. cocoa
1 tsp. vanilla

Bring to a boil in 9x13 inch pan.

Cake:

¾ c. sugar
¾ tsp. soda
3 Tbsp. cocoa
1½ c. flour

½ tsp. salt
3 Tbsp. shortening
¾ c. milk

Beat together and drop in hot liquid. Bake at 375° for 20 to 25 minutes.

Thelma Bland, Kansas

KANSAS DIRT CAKE

1½ lb. Oreo cookie crumbs
½ c. butter
1 c. milk
1 tsp. vanilla

18 oz. cream cheese
2 large containers whipped topping
2 (3½ oz.) vanilla instant pudding

Blend cookies in blender. Place ½ of crumbs in pan. Mix cream cheese, butter, and powdered sugar. Fold in 1 whipped topping. Mix milk and instant pudding. Fold into the cream cheese mixture. Pour over cookie crumbs. Top with second whipped topping and remaining cookie crumbs.

Bunny Adams, Kansas

GERMAN APPLE CAKE
(Excellent)

Crust:

1½ c. flour
½ tsp. salt
½ c. shortening

1 tsp. vanilla
2 to 3 Tbsp. ice water

Filling:

1 c. sugar
¼ c. flour
2 tsp. cinnamon

6 c. sliced peeled baking apples
1 c. heavy cream (whipping)

In a bowl, combine flour and salt; cut in shortening until mixture resembles coarse crumbs. Sprinkle with vanilla and stir in. Sprinkle with water, 1 tablespoon at a time, stirring until pastry holds together. Shape into a ball. On lightly floured surface, roll the dough to ⅛ inch thickness. Transfer to pie plate. Trim and flute edges.

Topping:

¼ c. flour
¼ c. sugar
¼ tsp. cinnamon

2 Tbsp. butter
¼ c. chopped nuts

Cut butter into mixture.

Filling: Combine ingredients in microwave-safe dish. Cook on HIGH, stirring occasionally, until apples are almost tender and filling is thickened. Cool. Pour into chilled shell. Sprinkle topping on. Bake in 400° oven for 10 to 15 minutes. Reduce heat to 350° and bake until crust is brown and apples are tender.

Marilyn Cowell, Missouri

NO ROLL PIE CRUST

1½ c. flour
1½ tsp. sugar

½ tsp. salt

Mix together in a 9 inch pie pan. Mix with fork until well blended. Beat together in a cup ½ cup salad oil with 2 tablespoons milk. Add to flour in pan. Mix until evenly dampened. Press out and up sides of pan with fingers. Bake in a 350° oven or use for pie as usual.

Can be doubled and divided and use the extra mixture for topping for fruit pies.

Marilyn Cowell, Missouri

PIE CRUST

2 c. flour
1 tsp. salt

⅔ c. Crisco
¼ c. water

Make paste ⅓ cup of the flour with ¼ cup water. Blend flour, salt, and Crisco. Add paste and roll.

Lois Redmann, Kentucky

BUTTERMILK PIE

Use raw 9 inch crust.

Filling - Cream:

2 Tbsp. flour
2 c. sugar

1 stick butter or margarine

Add 3 eggs. Mix well. Add 1 cup buttermilk. Bake at 425° for 10 minutes, then turn down the heat to 325° and bake for 50 minutes.

Nancy Matlock, Indiana

OUT OF THIS WORLD PIE

1 can cherry pie filling
¾ c. sugar
1 large can crushed pineapple and
   juice
1 Tbsp. cornstarch

1 tsp. red food coloring
1 (3 oz.) box raspberry gelatin
6 bananas, sliced
1 c. chopped pecans
1 large baked pie shell

In a saucepan, combine cherry pie filling, sugar, pineapple and juice, cornstarch, and food coloring. Cook until thick. Remove from heat and add gelatin. Allow to cool. Add bananas and pecans. Pour into pie shells and top with whipped topping. Chill.

Dorothy Foels, Iowa

BLUEBERRY PIE

Have on hand 1 graham cracker crust. (If homemade, use 10 inch glass pie pan.) Cover with 2 to 3 sliced bananas. Sprinkle each layer with lemon juice.

Beat:

1 (8 oz.) pkg. cream cheese
½ c. sugar

1 tsp. vanilla

Fold in one 12 ounce carton Cool Whip. Spread cream mixture over bananas. Combine 1 pint washed fresh or frozen blueberries with 1 can blueberry pie filling. Chill. Garnish with a little Cool Whip and sprig of mint. Can be frozen.

Carole Burke, Iowa

RHUBARB PIE

3 c. rhubarb, diced
3 eggs
1½ c. sugar

3 Tbsp. flour
¼ tsp. salt
2 Tbsp. milk

Mix together and pour into unbaked double pie crust. Bake 10 minutes at 400° and 35 to 40 minutes at 375°.

Lois J. Whitehead, Iowa

GRANDMA'S COTTAGE CHEESE PIE

Beat 3 eggs well and then add 2 cups cottage cheese and ¾ cup sugar. Mix well. Add 1 teaspoon vanilla and 1 cup milk. Pour into unbaked pie shell. Put in 375° oven for 15 minutes, then reduce heat to 350° until set.

Irene Krull, Florida

PEACH COBBLER

4 c. fresh peaches, peeled and
   sliced or chopped
1 c. sugar
½ c. (1 stick) margarine

2 c. sugar
1½ c. flour
4 tsp. baking powder
1½ c. milk

Combine fresh fruit and first 1 cup sugar. Set aside. Melt 1 stick margarine in 9x13 inch pan. Mix remaining 2 cups sugar, flour, baking powder, and milk. Pour this batter over melted margarine. Do not stir. Spoon fruit over batter. Do not stir. Bake at 325° about an hour until lightly browned.

For a change, you can use other fruit (berries or cherries).

Mrs. Dorothy Pfingsten, Illinois

ENGLISH PIE

1 c. sugar
½ c. butter
2 eggs, separated
1 c. raisins

1 c. chopped pecans
1 tsp. vanilla
1 pastry crust

Combine sugar and butter; add egg yolks, raisins, and pecans. Beat egg whites until stiff; fold into filling. Fold in vanilla. Pour into pastry shell. Bake at 350° until done. (Check by inserting toothpick in center of pie.) Yield: 6 servings.

Jan Bell, Iowa

YOGURT PIE

1 (8 oz.) container strawberry yogurt
1 (8 oz.) container Cool Whip

Graham cracker crust

Fold 1 (8 ounce) container strawberry yogurt into 1 (8 ounce) container of Cool Whip. Spoon into a graham cracker crust. Freeze until firm (about 4 hours). Remove from freezer about 30 minutes before serving.

May use lemon or blueberry yogurt.

Wanda Earp, Texas

FRUITY PIE

3 Tbsp. tapioca
1 c. sugar or 4 tsp. Sweet 'N Low
½ c. flour or 4 egg whites or 2 eggs
1 c. raisins or blueberries

1 qt. or 4 c. apples or favorite fruit
1 pie shell
1 tsp. apple pie spice

Stir ingredients together. Pour into pie shell. Bake at 350° for 25 to 30 minutes.

High fiber! No sugar (optional). No eggs (optional).

Renee Helphingstine, Kansas

TURTLE PIE

Have on hand 9 inch baked and cooled pie shell.

Filling:

36 caramels

½ c. whipped cream

Combine caramels and cream. Heat slowly until melted. Stir in 3½ cups pecan halves.

Topping:

1 tsp. butter

¼ c. chocolate chips

Melt butter and chips slowly, stirring constantly. Add 1 tablespoon cream and blend. Drizzle over filled pie.

Burton-Carolyn Fruechte, Minnesota

BUTTERSCOTCH PIE

2 c. brown sugar
2 c. milk
4 egg yolks

1 stick butter
1½ tsp. vanilla
4 Tbsp. flour

In iron skillet, melt butter on medium heat. Mix brown sugar and flour. Add to melted butter. Stir and cook for 1 minute. Mix egg yolks, milk, and vanilla. Add to brown sugar and stir all the time it is cooking. When thick, turn off heat and stir until smooth. Pour into 9 inch baked pie shell. Top with meringue. Bake until delicately browned.

Georgiann Pickens, Indiana

MOM'S LEMON PIE

3 eggs, separated
¾ c. sugar
3 Tbsp. flour
1 lemon

¾ c. water
2 Tbsp. butter
9 tsp. sugar
½ tsp. vanilla

Separate eggs. Put yolks in saucepan and whites in dry bowl to be used for meringue. Put sugar, flour, water, margarine or butter, and juice from lemon along with the egg yolks over medium heat. Stir. When it comes to a boil, remove and put in baked pie crust.

Beat egg whites till they are stiff. Add sugar and vanilla. Beat again so that you can turn upside down and it stays in peaks. Put over lemon pie and bake till golden brown, about 15 minutes, in a 350° oven.

Lois Redmann, Kentucky

CHOCOLATE DROP COOKIES

1 c. brown sugar
½ c. shortening
1 egg
½ c. milk
½ tsp. soda
1½ c. sifted flour

¼ tsp. salt
2 sq. unsweetened chocolate,
   melted
1 tsp. vanilla
½ c. nutmeats

Cream sugar and shortening. Add egg and beat. Combine flour, salt, and soda. Add sifted ingredients alternately with milk. Add melted chocolate and mix well. Add nuts. Drop from teaspoon onto greased cookie sheet. Bake at 350° for 10 to 12 minutes. When cool, frost with powdered sugar icing. Makes about 3 dozen cookies.

Letha Heichel, Iowa

WHEATIES COOKIES

1 c. shortening	1 tsp. soda
1 c. white sugar	1/2 tsp. salt
1 c. brown sugar	1 tsp. vanilla
2 eggs	2 c. Quaker Oats
2 c. flour	2 c. Wheaties
1/2 tsp. baking powder	1 c. coconut

Cream together shortening, sugars, and eggs. Add flour, baking powder, soda, and salt. After blended, add oats, Wheaties, coconut, and vanilla. Bake 10 minutes at 350°.

Donna J. Buss, Nebraska

MOLASSES CRINKLES COOKIES

3/4 c. shortening	1 egg
1 c. brown sugar	1/4 c. molasses

Mix together.

Add to mixture:

2 1/2 c. flour	1/4 tsp. salt
2 tsp. soda	1 tsp. ginger
1/2 tsp. cloves	1 tsp. cinnamon

Chill dough. Roll into balls. Dip into water and then into sugar. Bake only until set (not brown) 7 minutes at 375°.

Ken and Gail Root, AgriTalk

FRUIT BAR COOKIES

2 1/2 c. sugar	3 eggs
2 tsp. salt	1 c. and 3 Tbsp. oleo
1/2 c. honey	4 tsp. soda
1 1/2 tsp. cinnamon	1 1/2 c. raisins or dates
Nutmeats	2 Tbsp. water
5 c. flour	

Mix soda in flour and add to rest of the ingredients, mixing well. Chill dough. Roll on floured cloth board. Roll in 2 inch wide rolls or strips or the width of 2 fingers. Flatten a little and place on cookie sheet. Bake at 350° until done. Test a few on the cookie sheet to see how long for your oven. Whip egg and spread on before baking. Let stand a few minutes after baking.

Margaret Courrier, Minnesota

GERMAN CHOCOLATE COOKIES

Topping:

1 c. sugar	3 egg yolks, beaten
1 c. evaporated milk	1 1/2 c. flaked coconut
1/2 c. butter or margarine, softened	1 1/2 c. chopped pecans
1 tsp. vanilla	

Cookies:

1 pkg. Pillsbury Plus German chocolate cake mix

⅓ c. butter or margarine, melted

In heavy 2 quart saucepan, combine sugar, milk, ½ cup butter, vanilla, and egg yolks; blend well. Cook over medium heat for 10 to 13 minutes or until thickened and bubbly, stirring frequently. Stir in coconut and pecans. Remove from heat. Cool to room temperature.

Reserve 1¼ cups of topping mixture; set aside. In large bowl, combine cookie ingredients and remaining topping mixture; stir by hand until thoroughly moistened.

Heat oven to 350°F. Shape dough into 1 inch balls. Place 2 inches apart on ungreased cookie sheets. With thumb, make an indentation in center of each ball. Fill each indentation with rounded ½ teaspoonful of reserved 1¼ cups topping. Bake at 350°F. for 10 to 13 minutes or until set. Cool 5 minutes; remove from cookie sheets. Cool completely. Makes about 5 dozen cookies.

The best cookies I have every made.

Sue McGaughey, South Dakota

DELICIOUS COOKIES

1 c. white sugar
1 c. brown sugar
1 c. margarine
1 c. cooking oil
1 egg
1 tsp. vanilla
1 tsp. salt
1 tsp. cream of tartar

1 tsp. soda
1 c. Rice Krispies
1 c. coconut
1 c. oatmeal
½ c. nuts
3½ c. flour
Chocolate chips

Blend sugars, margarine, oil, egg, and vanilla. Add flour, salt, soda, and cream of tartar. Add remaining ingredients. Drop by spoon. Press down with fork or hands. Bake in a 350° oven for 12 to 15 minutes. Makes about 100 cookies.

Alice Oehler, Wisconsin

WHITE SUGAR COOKIES

1 c. butter, softened
1 c. oil
1 c. powdered sugar
1 c. sugar
2 eggs

1 tsp. vanilla
1 tsp. baking soda
1 tsp. cream of tartar
4 c. plus 4 tsp. flour, sifted

Cream butter, oil, and sugars. Add eggs and vanilla; beat well. Sift together baking soda, cream of tartar, and flour. Add to creamed mixture. Drop by teaspoon onto greased baking sheets, then flatten slightly with glass dipped in granulated sugar. Bake at 325° for about 15 minutes until light brown around edges. Decorate with colored sugar for Christmas cookies.

Shirley Hummel, Wisconsin; Frances Fuchs, Minnesota

RAW PEANUT COOKIES

1 c. brown sugar
1 c. white sugar
1 c. margarine
2 eggs
1 tsp. vanilla
1 c. crushed corn flakes

1 c. quick oats
1 c. raw Spanish peanuts
2 c. flour
1 tsp. baking powder
1 tsp. soda
¼ tsp. salt

Combine sugars, margarine, and eggs. Mix well. Add remaining ingredients. Drop by teaspoonfuls on cookie sheet and bake in a 350°F. oven for 8 minutes.

Marlys Marshall, Iowa

MOLASSES COOKIES

¾ c. shortening
1 c. brown sugar
1 egg
4 Tbsp. molasses (green label)
¼ tsp. salt

2¼ c. flour (I only use 2 c.)
2 tsp. soda
½ tsp. cloves (¼ tsp. is plenty)
½ tsp. cinnamon
¾ tsp. ginger

Refrigerate dough for several hours. Roll in balls. Dip in sugar and bake in moderate oven 8 to 10 minutes. Press down with glass dipped in sugar.

Thomas Luhman, Iowa

FRUIT BAR COOKIES

2½ c. sugar
2 tsp. salt
½ c. honey
1½ tsp. cinnamon
Nutmeats
5 c. flour

3 eggs
1 c. and 3 Tbsp. oleo
4 tsp. soda
1½ c. raisins or dates
2 Tbsp. water

Mix soda in flour and add to rest of the ingredients, mixing well. Chill dough. Roll on floured cloth board. Roll in 2 inch wide rolls or strips or the width of 2 fingers. Flatten a little and place on cookie sheet. Bake at 350° until done. Test a few on the cookie sheet to see how long for your oven. Whip egg and spread on before baking. Let stand a few minutes after baking.

Margaret Courrier, Minnesota

CAKE MIX CRINKLES
(Cookies)

1 box dry cake mix
4 oz. Cool Whip

3 Tbsp. oil
1 egg

Mix to form dough. Make 1 inch balls and roll in sugar. Place 2 inches apart on a cookie sheet. Bake at 350° for 10 to 12 minutes. Makes 3½ dozen.

I use strawberry or cherry cake mix and roll in red sugar.

Estamae Williams, Illinois

ICEBOX COOKIES
(Old family recipe)

1 c. margarine
1 c. lard
1 c. white sugar
1 c. dark Karo syrup
2 tsp. baking soda

2 Tbsp. hot water
5 c. flour
2 tsp. cinnamon
1 c. chopped walnuts

Mix all thoroughly. Roll up in waxed paper. Make rolls about 1 foot long each or less. They should be rectangular for the diameter. Refrigerate until firm and slice ¼ inch thick. Bake at 350° until lightly browned. The rolls will last in the refrigerator for many weeks.

Susan Conner, Iowa

WHITE CHIP ORANGE DREAM COOKIES

2¼ c. flour
¾ tsp. baking soda
1 c. butter
½ c. white sugar
½ c. brown sugar

1 egg
2 c. white Nestle morsels
¼ tsp. salt
1 to 2 tsp. orange peel, grated

Cream sugars and butter. Add egg, orange peel, soda, salt, and flour. Stir in morsels. Drop dough on ungreased sheet. Bake at 350° for 10 to 12 minutes. Let stand 2 minutes. Remove and cool.

Carole Burke, Iowa

BANANA JUMBOS

1 c. shortening
1 c. sugar
2 eggs
1 c. mashed bananas (2 to 3)
½ c. buttermilk

1 tsp. vanilla
3 c. flour
1½ tsp. baking soda
½ tsp. salt
1 c. nuts, chopped

Mix shortening, sugar, and eggs real well. Add bananas, milk, and vanilla. Combine dry ingredients. Add to banana mixture and stir well. Chill 1 hour. Drop onto cookie sheets. Bake at 350° about 8 minutes.

If you don't have buttermilk, use ½ cup milk with 1 teaspoon lemon juice. Let sit for 10 minutes, then add.

Mark and Cathy Perrin, AgriTalk

WHITE COOKIES

1½ c. shortening
1½ c. granulated sugar
2 eggs
1 tsp. vanilla

½ c. sour milk (1½ tsp. lemon juice
   to ½ c. milk)
4½ c. sifted flour
1 tsp. soda

Cream shortening and sugar. Add eggs and vanilla. Mix soda in the sour milk and add alternately with flour to mixture. Chill thoroughly. Roll, cut, and bake at 350°F. for 8 to 10 minutes on a greased cookie sheet.

This recipe was my great-grandmothers.

Etta Winter, New York

PRIDE OF IOWA COOKIES

1 c. brown sugar	2 c. flour
1 c. white sugar	1 tsp. soda
1 c. shortening	1 tsp. baking powder
2 eggs	1/2 tsp. salt
1 c. coconut	1 tsp. vanilla
3 c. quick rolled oats	1 c. chopped nuts

Beat eggs in mixing bowl. Add sugar and softened shortening. Mix well. Add coconut, nuts, and vanilla. Sift and measure flour. Add salt, baking powder, and soda to mixture, then add rolled oats. Mix thoroughly. Roll in small balls the size of a walnut. Press down on cookie sheet and crease with fork. Bake at 375° for 9 minutes.

Lauretta Van Buskirk, Iowa

MONSTER COOKIES

2/3 c. butter	4 tsp. baking soda
2/3 c. margarine	1 c. flour
2 1/2 c. brown sugar	12 c. oatmeal
1 1/2 c. sugar	12 oz. pkg. chocolate chips
6 eggs	1 lb. M&M's
28 oz. jar peanut butter	

Cream together butter, margarine, and sugars. Add eggs and mix. Mix in peanut butter. Add flour and soda. In large bowl, mix oatmeal, chips, and M&M's. Work first mixture into the oatmeal mixture. Bake in 350° oven. Do not overbake. Makes a large batch.

Rose Breitsprecher, Minnesota

SUPREME RASPBERRY OATMEAL COOKIES

1/2 c. granulated sugar	1/2 c. butter Crisco or oleo

Cream together.

1 egg, beaten	1/2 tsp. vanilla

Add to creamed butter and sugar.

1/2 tsp. soda	1 c. all-purpose flour
1/2 tsp. baking powder	1/2 tsp. salt

Add to creamed mixture.

1/2 c. raspberry jam	1 c. quick oatmeal

Add to preceding. Drop in rounded tablespoons on greased baking sheet. Bake at 375° for 15 minutes. Yield: 2 1/2 dozen.

Myrtle Erickson, Iowa

DOUBLE TREAT COOKIES

2 c. flour
2 tsp. baking powder
1/2 tsp. salt
1 c. shortening
1 c. sugar
1 c. brown sugar

2 eggs
1 tsp. vanilla
1 c. peanut butter
1 c. chopped salted peanuts
1 (6 oz.) pkg. chocolate chips

Sift together dry ingredients. Beat next 5 ingredients until fluffy. Blend in peanut butter and add dry ingredients. Stir in peanuts and chocolate chips. Shape into small balls and place on ungreased baking sheet. Flatten with glass dipped in sugar. Bake at 350° for 8 minutes or until brown. Makes 7 dozen.

Frances Schott, Illinois

MINIATURE PEANUT BUTTER TREATS

Cookie:

1/2 c. butter, softened
1/2 c. brown sugar, packed
1/2 c. granulated sugar
1 egg
1/2 c. cream-style peanut butter

1/2 tsp. vanilla
1 1/4 c. flour
3/4 tsp. baking soda
1/2 tsp. salt

Filling: Have on hand 36 miniature peanut butter/chocolate cups.

Combine butter, sugars, egg, peanut butter, and vanilla in mixing bowl; beat until smooth. Combine flour, soda, and salt; add to creamed mixture. Roll in small balls and place each in miniature muffin tin.

With thumb, make a "well" or depression in each cookie. Bake at 375° for 8 minutes. Remove from oven; immediately place 1 peanut butter cup in each. Cool in pan for 10 minutes. Twist gently to remove from pan. Cool on rack. Store in cool place until serving time. Yield: 36 cookies.

Marlene Fudge, Indiana

FUDGE PUDDLES

1/2 c. butter or margarine, softened
1/2 c. creamy peanut butter
1/2 c. sugar
1/2 c. packed brown sugar
1 egg

1/2 tsp. vanilla extract
1 1/4 c. flour
3/4 tsp. baking soda
1/2 tsp. salt

Fudge Filling:

1 c. milk chocolate chips
1 c. semi-sweet chocolate chips
1 can sweetened condensed milk

1 tsp. vanilla extract
Chopped peanuts

Cream butter, peanut butter, and sugars; add egg and vanilla. Sift together flour, baking soda, and salt; add to creamed mixture. Mix well. Chill for 1 hour. Shape into 48 balls, 1 inch each. Place in lightly greased mini muffin tins. Bake at 325° for 14 to 16 minutes or until lightly browned. Remove from oven and immediately make "wells" in the center of each by lightly pressing with a melon baller. Cool in pans for 5 minutes, then carefully remove.

For filling, melt chocolate chips in a double boiler over simmering water. Stir in condensed milk and vanilla; mix well. Using a small pitcher or pastry bag, fill each shell with filling. Sprinkle with peanuts. (Leftover filling can be stored in the refrigerator and served warm over ice cream.) Yields 4 dozen.

"This is one of our favorite Christmas treats."

Robin Miedema, North Dakota

APPLE TURNOVERS (40)

5 c. flour
2 c. + 2 Tbsp. lard (or 2 c. Crisco
   plus 2 Tbsp. butter)
1 tsp. salt

1 pkg. yeast, dissolved in 1 c. warm
   milk (let stand 10 minutes)
2 eggs, beaten
¾ c. evaporated milk (or half & half)

Dissolve yeast in warm milk and let stand 10 minutes, then add beaten eggs and evaporated milk. Mix all together with flour mixture. Refrigerate overnight.

Filling:

1½ c. or less sugar
15 large apples
1 Tbsp. cinnamon

1 Tbsp. tapioca
1½ Tbsp. flour

Put mixture into 9x13 inch cake pan. Cook in slow oven until tender. Stir once in a while. Roll dough about ⅛ inch thick. Use a 2 pound coffee can as dough cutter. Place filling on dough. Fold over and seal with a fork. I brush with milk and sprinkle with sugar. Bake for 20 minutes at 375° or until lightly browned.

If you want to bake them later, lay flat on cookie sheet and freeze. Do not thaw before baking.

Irene Handzus, Minnesota

RHUBARB MERINGUE SQUARES

A tangy, fresh, delicious dessert in 3 layers.

Crust:

1 c. flour
1½ tsp. sugar

½ c. margarine

Heat oven to 375°. In a bowl, combine crust ingredients until crumbly. Press into ungreased 10x7 inch pan. Bake 15 minutes until golden.

Filling:

1½ c. sugar
2 Tbsp. cornstarch
3 c. rhubarb, diced
½ c. milk

¼ c. orange juice
3 egg yolks, slightly beaten (keep
   whites)

Combine filling ingredients, except egg yolks, in a saucepan. Cook over medium heat until rhubarb is tender and mixture has thickened, stirring constantly. Remove from heat. Stir small amount of hot mixture into egg yolks and add to cooked rhubarb. Return to burner and heat just until filling begins to boil or bubble. Set aside to cool.

Meringue:

3 egg whites
¼ tsp. cream of tartar

3 Tbsp. sugar
1 tsp. vanilla

Reduce oven temperature to 350°. Beat egg whites and cream of tartar until foamy. Beat in sugar, 1 tablespoon at a time. Continue beating until stiff and glossy. Don't underbeat. Beat in vanilla.

Pour slightly cooled filling over crust. Spread meringue on top, sealing edges. Bake 12 to 15 minutes, until meringue is golden brown. Serves 6 to 8.

Lois J. Whitehead, Iowa

TING-A-LINGS

1 (6 oz.) pkg. chocolate chips

1 (6 oz.) pkg. butterscotch chips

Place in a double boiler and melt chips slowly.

When softened, add:

1 c. salted peanuts
1 c. coconut

1 c. chow mein noodles

Mix together and drop on wax paper by spoonfuls.

Mrs. Germaine Winter, Iowa

EASY FUDGE

1 c. chocolate chips
2 c. butterscotch chips
¼ c. butter

1 (14 oz.) can sweetened condensed milk

Mix all together. Microwave them 3 or 5 minutes to soften. Stir and add 1 cup any kind of nuts. Spread into a greased 9 inch pan. Chill. *Good.*

Almeda Eickhoff, Minnesota

HO-HO BARS

½ c. oleo
½ c. oil
1 c. water
½ c. buttermilk

1 tsp. soda
3 Tbsp. cocoa
2 c. flour

Mix and pour in a brownie pan. Bake 25 minutes at 350°.

Filling:

1 c. sugar
1 c. Crisco
½ tsp. salt

½ c. milk
1 Tbsp. water
1 tsp. vanilla

Beat ingredients 5 minutes and add 1 cup powdered sugar. Spread over cooled cake.

106

Frosting:

1 c. sugar
½ c. milk

6 Tbsp. oleo

Boil 1 minute and add 1½ cups chocolate chips. Beat until cool and frost the cake.

Evelyn Struwe, South Dakota

COFFEE HOUR LEMON BARS

1 box yellow cake mix
⅓ c. oil
2 eggs
8 oz. cream cheese, softened

⅓ c. lemon juice, freshly squeezed
½ tsp. lemon zest (finely grated rind of lemon)

Preheat oven to 350°. Mix together cake mix, oil, and 1 egg until the mixture becomes crumbly. Reserve 1 cup of this mixture for topping. Put the remaining into a 9x12 inch pan and bake 12 to 15 minutes.

Meanwhile, beat softened cream cheese with sugar. Add 1 egg and lemon zest and juice. Beat until very light and fluffy. Spread over baked crust and top with reserved cake crumb mixture. Bake for another 15 minutes, until lightly browned on top. Cool well before cutting into squares.

Ingalls, South Dakota

NO MIX CHERRY DESSERT

½ c. margarine
½ c. flour
½ c. sugar
1 tsp. baking powder

¼ tsp. salt
½ c. milk
1 can cherry or any kind of pie filling

Melt margarine in 8x8 inch glass pan. Mix flour, sugar, baking powder, salt, and milk. Pour over melted margarine. Do not mix. Spoon pie filling over mixture. Do not mix. Bake at 350° for 45 to 50 minutes. Serve hot or cold.

Mary Berger, South Dakota

VALENTINE DELIGHT

1 stick oleo (½ c.)
1¼ c. flour

2 tsp. sugar (white or brown)
1 tsp. salt

Combine and bake in a 9x13 inch glass pan until brown. Stir occasionally until brown. Cool.

In a large mixer bowl, beat:

1 (10 oz.) pkg. strawberries
1 c. white sugar

2 Tbsp. lemon juice
2 egg whites

Beat 20 minutes (yes 20 minutes) on high speed, then fold in a 9 ounce container Cool Whip. Put ⅔ cup of crumbs on bottom of 9x13 inch pan. Pour strawberry mixture on top, then add remaining crumbs on top of strawberry mixture. Freeze. Serve frozen. *Yummy.*

Rosalie Nelsen, Nebraska

GINGER BALLS

¾ c. shortening
1 c. sugar
1 egg
4 Tbsp. molasses
1 tsp. salt

2 c. flour
2 tsp. soda
1 tsp. cinnamon
½ tsp. cloves
1 tsp. ginger

Cream sugar and oleo. Add egg and molasses. Beat well. Mix spices and soda with flour and add to the first mixture. Roll in balls (less than an inch). Roll top in sugar. Bake at 350° for 12 to 15 minutes.

Ruth Kenaley, Iowa

EGGNOG LOGS

¾ c. sugar
1 c. oleo
2 tsp. vanilla
2 tsp. rum extract

1 egg
3 c. flour and 1 tsp. nutmeg, mixed
together

Cream sugar and oleo well. Add flavorings and egg. Mix well. Stir in dry ingredients. Divide dough and roll into long rope, about ½ inch in diameter. Cut into 3 inch lengths. Bake at 350° for 12 to 15 minutes.

Frosting:

2 c. powdered sugar
3 Tbsp. oleo
¾ tsp. rum extract

¼ tsp. vanilla
2 to 3 Tbsp. half & half or milk

Frost top and sides of logs and sprinkle with nutmeg. Store in tightly covered container.

Ruth Kenaley, Iowa

VELVEETA CHEESE FUDGE

1 lb. butter
1 lb. Velveeta cheese
4 lb. powdered sugar

1 c. cocoa
1 Tbsp. vanilla
1½ c. nuts (optional)

Melt butter and cheese until smooth. Mix cocoa and sugar; add cheese mixture. Add nuts and vanilla. Mix well. Pour into greased pan. Cool and cut. This will make 6½ pounds.

A creamy and udderly delicious fudge. Can reduce this recipe to smaller batch very easily.

Ardes Montanye, Minnesota

CARAMEL OATMEAL CHEWS

The 1995 champion prize winner at American Beekeeping Federation Ladies Auxiliary in Austin, Texas.

1½ c. flour
¾ c. margarine
½ c. brown sugar
½ c. honey
2 c. uncooked oatmeal

½ tsp. baking soda
1 pkg. caramels
1 can sweetened and condensed milk
½ c. chopped nuts

Mix together first 6 ingredients and put ⅔ on large, greased cookie sheet. Bake 10 minutes at 350°. Melt caramels and milk over medium heat. Pour over baked crust. Sprinkle with nuts and rest of crumbs. Bake 15 minutes longer, but do not overbake.

Ellen Sundberg, Minnesota

APPLE TURNOVERS

5 c. flour
1 c. shortening
1 tsp. salt
1 c. milk

1 small can condensed milk
1 pkg. yeast
2 eggs
4 Tbsp. sugar for rolling out

Mix flour, shortening, and salt like pie crust. Scald milk. Add condensed milk. When cool, soak yeast in liquid. Add beaten eggs. Mix flour into liquid. Chill a few hours. Take dough the size of an egg and roll with sugar pancake size and fill with apples, sweetened. Fold and seal. Bake at 375° for 25 minutes.

Irene Francheck, North Dakota

POTATO CANDY

1 medium potato
2 boxes powdered sugar

? peanut butter

In saucepan, boil a potato until done. Peel and cut into chunks. Mash. Add a box of powdered sugar while mashing until it forms a dough. (The hotter the potato, the more sugar it will take, so let it cool a little.) Sugar a flat surface and roll out. Spread with peanut butter. Roll like a jelly roll and slice ¼ inch thick. Place on wax paper, *not* touching each other, and refrigerate.

It tastes like peanut butter fudge. It looks like a pinwheel.

Estamae Williams, Illinois

BANANA BARS

2½ c. flour
1⅔ c. sugar
1¼ tsp. baking powder
1¼ tsp. soda
1 tsp. salt

¾ c. butter or margarine, softened
¾ c. buttermilk or sour milk
1¼ c. (3 medium) very ripe bananas, mashed

Mix dry ingredients thoroughly with the butter, buttermilk, and bananas. Add 2 eggs and beat 2 minutes. Add ½ cup chopped pecans. Put batter in an ungreased

10x12x1 inch pan. Bake at 350° for 25 to 30 minutes. When cooled, frost with the following.

Frosting:

4 c. sifted powdered sugar
½ c. butter or oleomargarine,
    softened

2 to 4 Tbsp. milk
2 tsp. vanilla
½ c. chopped pecans

Beat 1½ minutes until fluffy. Fold in pecans.

This recipe freezes well, before you frost it. A great way to use your overripe bananas.

Maxine Soppe, Wyoming

BROWNIES

1 c. white sugar
½ c. butter
4 eggs

1 large can chocolate syrup
1 c. flour
½ c. nuts

Bake in 9x13 inch pan at 350° for 30 to 35 minutes.

Frosting:

1½ c. sugar
6 tsp. milk

1 tsp. butter

Mix and boil 1 minute. Add ¾ cup chocolate chips. Beat until melted. Spread over brownies.

Pauline Wendling, Wisconsin

OH HENRY BARS

4 c. quick cooking oats
1 c. shortening
½ c. white corn syrup
1 tsp. vanilla

¾ c. peanut butter
1 c. brown sugar
½ tsp. salt
1 (12 oz.) pkg. chocolate bits

Preheat oven to 350°. In a large bowl, combine oats, sugar, shortening, and syrup, using a pastry blender. Press into a 9x13 inch pan. Bake 15 minutes. Cool slightly. Melt chocolate chips and peanut butter. Spread over baked mixture. Cool slightly and cut into bars. Refrigerate.

Marlene Fudge, Indiana

PEANUT BUTTER KRISPIES

1 c. sugar
1 c. white sugar

1 c. peanut butter
5 c. Rice Krispies cereal

Bring sugar and syrup to a boil. Remove from stove. Stir in peanut butter till melted. Mix in cereal and spread into a well buttered cookie sheet. Cool and cut into squares.

Breanne Childs, Illinois

EASY CHEESY BROWNIES

1 c. butter or oleo	2 tsp. vanilla
4 (1 oz.) sq. semi-sweet chocolate	1½ c. flour
2 c. sugar	½ tsp. salt
4 eggs	1 c. chopped nuts

Cream Cheese Filling:

1 (8 oz.) pkg. cream cheese, softened	1 egg
¼ c. sugar	1½ tsp. vanilla

Beat all ingredients for Cream Cheese Filling in small mixer bowl on medium speed. Scrape sides occasionally. Set aside. Melt butter and chocolate in small pan on low heat. Stir occasionally. Cool.

Beat chocolate mixture, sugar, eggs, and vanilla in large mixing bowl on medium speed for about 1 minute. Beat in flour and salt on low speed for about ½ minute, then beat on medium speed for 1 minute. Stir in nuts.

Spread ½ the dough in 9x13 inch pan, then spread the Cream Cheese Filling over the first layer. Gently spread the remaining half of dough over the Cream Cheese Filling. Gently swirl over and under motion for marbled effect. Bake 30 or 35 minutes in 350° oven or until wooden pick comes out clean. Cut in squares.

Kay Cross, Missouri

PEANUT BUTTER FINGERS

Cream:

½ c. oleo	½ c. brown sugar
½ c. sugar	

Blend in:

1 egg	¼ tsp. salt
⅓ c. peanut butter	½ tsp. vanilla
½ tsp. soda	

Stir in:

1 c. flour	1 c. oatmeal

Spread in greased 13x9 inch pan and bake at 350° for 20 to 25 minutes. Spread one 6 ounce package chocolate chips over this. Let stand 5 minutes.

Combine:

½ c. powdered sugar	2 to 4 Tbsp. evaporated milk
¼ c. peanut butter	

Mix well. Spread chocolate evenly. Drizzle with peanut butter mixture. Cool. Cut in bars.

LaVern Kraft, Iowa

CHOCOLATE GOODIE

½ c. margarine
1 c. flour
1 c. pecans
1 (8 oz.) pkg. Cool Whip
1 (8 oz.) pkg. cream cheese
1 c. powdered sugar

1 (3 oz.) pkg. instant chocolate pudding
1 (3 oz.) pkg. instant vanilla pudding
3 c. milk

1. Mix together ½ cup margarine, 1 cup flour, and 1 cup pecans. Spread into a 9x13 inch pan. Bake at 350° for 15 minutes. Cool.
2. Beat until creamy 4½ ounces Cool Whip, one 8 ounce package cream cheese, and 1 cup powdered sugar. Pour onto cooled crust.
3. Mix together one 3 ounce package instant chocolate pudding, one 3 ounce package vanilla instant pudding, and 3 cups milk. Pour over the cream cheese layer.
4. Top with 4½ ounces Cool Whip.
5. Chill.

Jessie Reilly, Texas

OLD-FASHIONED RICE PUDDING

½ c. rice
4 c. milk
½ tsp. salt

½ c. sugar
Cinnamon

In a 2½ quart casserole, combine rice, milk, salt, and sugar. Bake in a slow oven (300°) for 2 to 3 hours, covered. Stir once during baking. Sprinkle with cinnamon (optional).

This recipe dates back to before the year 1940.

Luella Suhr, Iowa

BREAD PUDDING

2 c. dry bread crumbs
½ c. granulated sugar
1 pt. cream or milk
4 eggs

¼ tsp. cinnamon
½ tsp. vanilla
4 Tbsp. butter
Salt

Soak bread crumbs in cream. Add sugar, butter, beaten eggs, and salt for flavoring. Place in a buttered baking dish and add a little chopped citron, chopped raisins, and dates. Bake about 40 minutes in a 350° oven.

This recipe dates back to before the year 1940.

Luella Suhr, Iowa

STEAMED BROWN PUDDING

⅓ c. lard
⅓ c. butter
1⅓ c. brown sugar
1 tsp. ground cinnamon
¾ tsp. ground cloves

½ tsp. baking soda
1 tsp. baking powder
1 c. cold water
3 c. flour
1 c. raisins

Make in small angel food cake pan. Steam over a covered pan of water 2½ hours or ½ hour in pressure cooker No. 5. May be reheated before served. Good with whipped cream.

Nancy Matlock, Rushville, Indiana

CHERRY PUDDING

1 c. sugar	2 tsp. baking powder
1 c. flour	½ tsp. salt

Sift together and work in 1 tablespoon butter. Stir in ⅔ cup milk and beat well. Spread in 8x12 inch Pyrex baking dish. Mix one No. 2 can sour cherries with 1 cup sugar. Pour over first mixture. Bake 45 minutes at 350°.

Apples may be used in place of cherries. May serve with a scoop of vanilla ice cream. Best served warm.

The cherry pudding recipe is an old one from my grandmother who was a farm wife on a Shelby County, Iowa farm for most of her adult life. My grandparents were married in 1908 and retired from farming in 1948.

Linda Marek, Iowa

VANILLA ICE CREAM

4 eggs	2 c. whipping cream
1¾ c. sugar	2 Tbsp. pure vanilla
7 c. whole milk	½ tsp. salt

Beat eggs until light. Add sugar gradually, beating until mixture thickens. Add remaining ingredients; mix thoroughly. Freeze in ice cream freezer.

Rose Freking, Minnesota

DANISH ABELSKIVER

3 egg yolks	1 tsp. baking powder
½ tsp. salt	1 tsp. soda
2 c. buttermilk*	3 egg whites
2 c. flour	2 tsp. sugar

Beat egg yolks. Add sugar, salt, and buttermilk. Add flour, baking powder, and soda. Fold in stiffly beaten egg whites. Bake in shortening in an Abelskiver pan (also know as a fritter pan). When half baked, turn with a fork or an ice pick and finish baking. Serve with sugar, syrup or jam.

* May use powdered buttermilk mixed as directions on can.

Evalyn Sievers, Iowa

MYSTERY PECAN DESSERT

Whip 3 egg whites. Add 1 cup sugar. Fold in. Beat slowly and fold in 1 cup chopped pecans. Mix ⅓ teaspoon baking powder and 24 crumbled Ritz crackers. Mix all together and put in pie pan. Bake at 350° until done.

Can be baked several days ahead. Top with Cool Whip topping.

Mrs. E.E. Gritton, Kansas

SOY PEANUT BUTTER BROWNIES

1/3 c. soy oil margarine
1/2 c. ground cooked soybeans
1 c. sugar
2 eggs
1 tsp. baking powder
1/2 tsp. vanilla

1 (6 oz.) pkg. semi-sweet chocolate
  bits
1/2 c. peanut butter
1/2 c. firmly packed brown sugar
1 c. flour
1/4 tsp. salt

Beat margarine or butter, peanut butter, and soybeans together until light. Gradually add sugars, creaming well. Add eggs, one at a time, beating well after each addition. Add flour, baking powder, and salt, mixing well. Add chocolate bits and vanilla. Spread mixture in well-greased 9 inch pan. Bake at 325°F. for 30 to 35 minutes. Cool and cut into squares. Makes 12 servings.

Nutritional value (per serving): 335 calories, 17 g fat, 46 mg cholesterol, 195 mg sodium, and 7 g protein.

Reprinted with permission from the Minnesota Soybean Research and Promotion Council.

APPLE PASTRY DESSERT

2 1/2 c. flour
1 c. shortening
1 c. corn flakes
1 tsp. cinnamon
8 to 10 tart apples, sliced (8 c.)

1 tsp. salt
1 egg yolk
1 c. sugar
1 egg white

Combine flour and salt; cut in shortening. Beat egg yolk in measuring cup; add enough milk to make 2/3 cup liquid. Stir into flour mixture. Roll half the dough to 17 x 12 inch rectangle; fit into a 15 1/2 x 10 1/2 inch jelly roll pan. Sprinkle with corn flakes; top with apples. Combine sugar and cinnamon; sprinkle on top. Roll remaining dough to 15 1/2 x 10 1/2 inch rectangle. Place over apples. Seal edges; cut slits in top. Beat egg white and brush on crust. Bake at 375° for 50 minutes.

Dorothy Schmitt, Iowa

RHUBARB DESSERT

Crust:

1 1/2 c. flour   2/3 c. oleomargarine

Combine well and pat into a 9x13 inch pan. Bake for 15 minutes at 325°.

Filling:

4 c. cut up rhubarb   1 1/2 c. sugar
3 Tbsp. cornstarch

Cook until thick and rhubarb is done. (If the sugar is allowed to stand over the rhubarb for a while it "draws out" the juice so there is no need to add water. Cook over low heat, though.) When it is done, set it aside to cool for awhile and then pour over cooled crust.

Third layer:

1 (8 oz.) tub Cool Whip   **1½ c. miniature marshmallows**

Mix and spread over cooled rhubarb filling.

Fourth layer:

1 (3 oz.) pkg. vanilla instant   **1½ c. milk**
pudding

Combine and spread over marshmallow layer. Refrigerate.

LuElla made a "thicker filling" by using 6 cups of cut-up rhubarb and a little more of the cornstarch. When it had cooked she stirred in ½ box of strawberry jello - which gave it a pretty pink color - and also 1 cup of crushed pineapple with its juice. *Delicious!*

Mrs. Raymond Swanson, Nebraska

MARSHMALLOW BARS

½ c. oleo   **1 tsp. vanilla**
¾ c. sugar   **¼ tsp. baking powder**
2 eggs   **2 Tbsp. cocoa**
¼ tsp. salt   **¾ c. flour**

Cream oleo and sugar. Beat in eggs and vanilla. Stir together flour, cocoa, baking powder, and salt. Stir in egg mixture and spread in greased 13x9 inch pan. Bake at 350° for 15 minutes. Take out of oven and sprinkle 2 cups miniature marshmallows evenly on top of bars. Put in oven for 2 or 3 minutes more and then cool.

In small saucepan, combine:

1 (6 oz.) pkg. chocolate chips   **1 c. peanut butter**

Slowly melt over low heat, stirring till chocolate chips are melted. Stir in 1½ cups of Rice Krispies and then spread this on top of cooled bars. Chill and cut into bars.

Nancy Buresh, North Dakota

FUDGE BARS

Bars:

½ c. margarine   **¾ c. flour**
1 c. brown sugar   **½ tsp. salt**
1 egg   **½ tsp. soda**
½ tsp. vanilla   **2 c. oatmeal**

Filling:

1 pkg. milk chocolate chips   **1 can sweetened condensed milk**
1 Tbsp. butter   **Pinch of salt**

Mix bar ingredients together and reserve ¾ to 1 cup for topping. Spread the remainder in a slightly greased 9x13 inch pan. Melt chocolate chips, butter, salt, and sweetened condensed milk together in microwave or double boiler until smooth. Put on first layer. Sprinkle with reserved topping. Bake at 350° for 20 to 25 minutes.

Jan E. Johansen, Iowa

EIGHT-MINUTE CHEESE

1 (8 oz.) pkg. cream cheese	1 (8 oz.) container whipped topping
1/3 c. sugar	2 tsp. vanilla
1 c. sour cream	Strawberries

In a 10 inch deep dish pie plate *or* 8 inch baking dish, make crust of graham crackers or vanilla wafers. Beat cheese until smooth, then add sugar gradually, beating in well. Blend in sour cream and vanilla. Fold in whipped topping. Spoon into crust. Chill for 2 hours. Garnish with strawberries.

Mrs. Shirley Sock, Nebraska

BROWNIES

2 sticks margarine	4 eggs
8 Tbsp. cocoa	2 c. flour
2 c. sugar	1 tsp. vanilla

In saucepan, melt margarine. Stir in cocoa. Let get very hot. Remove from heat, then add sugar, next the eggs, flour, and vanilla. You can add nuts. Stir till mixed. Bake in 9x13 inch pan at 350° for 25 minutes. Don't overbake brownies.

Christena Gasner, Minnesota

SPIFFEY CHERRY DESSERT

Mix:

2 c. vanilla wafers, crushed	1/3 c. melted butter

Save 2 tablespoons for topping. Spread in pan.

Mix:

1/2 c. butter, creamed	1 1/2 c. powdered sugar

Add 2 eggs, one at a time. Beat well. Spread over crumbs.

Top with:

1 c. heavy cream, whipped, or Cool Whip	2 Tbsp. cocoa
	1/4 c. sugar

Add:

1/4 c. cut up cherries (maraschino)	1 mashed banana
1 c. nutmeats, chopped	

Top with remaining crumbs.

Mrs. Donald Traver, Iowa

EDNA'S RHUBARB PUDDING

Mix:

1 c. sugar	1 c. flour
1½ tsp. baking powder	¾ c. milk

Pour over 1 stick oleo in square baking dish. Put 3 cups chopped rhubarb on top of batter. Sprinkle ¾ cup sugar over all. *Do not stir.* Bake at 350° till brown.

Grace Fisher, Missouri

CHERRY-MARSHMALLOW BARS

¾ c. margarine, melted	¼ c. water
⅓ c. brown sugar	¼ tsp. cherry flavoring
1¼ c. flour	½ tsp. vanilla flavoring
2 pkg. unflavored gelatin	½ c. maraschino cherries, drained
½ c. water	and chopped
2 c. sugar	Coconut
¼ c. maraschino juice	

Combine margarine, brown sugar, and flour and blend well. Press into greased 9x13 inch pan. Bake at 325° for 20 minutes. Cool. Combine unflavored gelatin and ½ cup water. Set aside.

In a saucepan, mix sugar, cherry juice, and remaining water. Bring to a boil and boil 2 to 4 minutes. Pour mixture over gelatin and beat at least 10 minutes. Add flavorings and cherries. Pour over baked layer. Sprinkle coconut on top. Cut in squares.

Irene Tiedtke, Nebraska

ALWAYS GOOD BROWNIES

½ c. melted oleo or butter	1 tsp. baking powder
1½ c. sugar	½ tsp. salt
3 eggs	1 tsp. vanilla
1 c. flour	½ tsp. burnt sugar flavoring
⅓ c. cocoa	½ to 1 c. chopped nuts

Mix melted butter and sugar. Cool. Add eggs and mix well with mixer. Add dry ingredients and beat on slow speed until mixed in. Add flavorings and nuts. Pour into greased 11 x 7½ inch pan. Bake in 350° oven for approximately 30 minutes. Test with toothpick. Watch carefully as this can overbake easily.

Louise Davis, Missouri

APPLE CRISP

3 c. apples	¾ c. flour
¼ c. sugar	½ c. sugar
½ c. water	½ margarine

Slice apples and put on bottom of pan. Sprinkle sugar and water over them. Mix flour, sugar, and butter together and put on top of apples. Sprinkle with cinnamon and walnuts if desired. Bake at 350° for 40 minutes.

Lois Redmann, Kentucky

DATE NUT PUDDING

¾ c. sugar
1 c. flour
2 tsp. baking powder

1 c. dates, finely diced
½ c. milk (a little more if needed)
½ c. pecans

Mix preceding ingredients thoroughly and spread in greased 9x13 inch pan.

Pour the following over the top:

1½ c. light brown sugar
2 Tbsp. butter or margarine

1½ c. hot water

Mix preceding until margarine is melted, then pour over the preceding. Bake in a 350° oven for approximately 35 minutes. If using glass pan, lower heat temperature to 325°. Should be light golden brown with caramel not thin in bottom. Serve with Cool Whip on top.

This was a recipe my mother always made at Thanksgiving and Christmas which we still do.

Margery Broers, Illinois

CHOCOLATE DATE SQUARES

2 c. chopped dates
1 c. sugar
2 eggs
1½ c. all-purpose flour

1 tsp. baking soda
1 c. hot water
⅔ c. shortening
½ tsp. salt

Topping:

1 c. (6 oz.) semi-sweet chocolate
 chips

½ c. brown sugar, packed
½ c. chopped nuts

In a bowl, combine dates and water; set aside to cool (do not drain). In a mixing bowl, cream sugar and shortening. Add eggs, flour, baking soda, and salt. Mix well. Add dates. Pour into greased and floured 13x9x2 inch baking pan.

Combine the topping ingredients. Sprinkle over batter. Bake at 350° for 40 minutes or until a wooden pick inserted in the center comes out clean. Yields 24 squares.

Johanna Kruse, Minnesota

WILMA'S CHERRY CRUMB

1½ c. flour
1½ c. oatmeal
⅔ c. butter or margarine

1¼ c. brown sugar
1 tsp. soda
½ tsp. salt

Mix preceding ingredients and pat ½ mixture into a 13x9 inch baking dish. Top with 2 cans cherry pie filling. Top with remaining crumb mixture. Bake at 350° for 45 minutes.

Linda Peterson, Minnesota

BREAD PUDDING

4 c. cubed (³/₄ inch) stale French
    bread*
¹/₂ c. raisins
3 c. milk, divided
3 Tbsp. packed brown sugar,
    divided
Pinch of salt

1 large egg
2 egg whites
¹/₃ c. granulated sugar
1 tsp. vanilla
¹/₂ tsp. cinnamon
¹/₄ tsp. nutmeg

Preheat oven to 350°F. Spray 8x8 inch baking pan. Scatter the bread cubes and the raisins into this. Combine the 2 cups of milk and the 2 tablespoons of brown sugar and the salt to dissolve the sugar. Pour over the bread cubes. Let stand for 15 minutes. Beat the whole egg and the egg whites with the ¹/₃ cup granulated sugar. Add the vanilla, cinnamon, nutmeg, and the remaining milk. Stir the bread cubes a little and pour the egg mixture over all. Sprinkle the remaining 1 tablespoon of brown sugar over the top. Bake 50 to 55 minutes or until a knife inserted 1 inch from the edge of the pan comes out clean. Remove from oven and set on a cooling rack to cool. Serve warm. Makes 8 servings. *Very good.*

* Don't use the bread you buy for sandwiches - use only firm bread.

Mildred Haas, Nebraska

MICRO-CREAMY RICE PUDDING

2¹/₂ c. milk
¹/₂ c. Minute rice
1 small pkg. vanilla pudding (not
    instant)

¹/₃ c. raisins
Dash of cinnamon

Mix together in a 2 quart container. Microwave on HIGH 6 to 8 minutes, stirring twice.

Gert Winter, Minnesota

CREAM CHEESE BROWNIES

1 box favorite brownie mix and
    ingredients listed
2 (8 oz.) pkg. cream cheese

¹/₂ c. butter or margarine
¹/₂ c. sugar
2 tsp. vanilla

Preheat oven to temperature noted on brownie mix. Prepare brownies as directed on package. The instructions for "cakelike brownies" generally works best for this recipe, but normal preparation will also give good results. Spread ¹/₂ of mixture in bottom of 13x9 inch cake pan (grease only bottom).

In small cook pan, over medium heat, melt butter. Add cream cheese and heat until cream cheese is warmed and can be mixed with the butter. Remove from heat; add the sugar and vanilla, mixing well. Spread cream cheese mixture on top of brownie mixture in cake pan. Spread remaining ¹/₂ of brownie mixture over this. Cook per instructions on brownie mix, adding approximately 5 more minutes.

Mary Godwin, Iowa

Notes

Miscellaneous

TEMPERATURE TESTS
FOR CANDY MAKING

There are two different methods of determining when candy has been cooked to the proper consistency. One is by using a candy thermometer in order to record degrees, the other is by using the cold water test. The chart below will prove useful in helping to follow candy recipes:

TYPE OF CANDY	DEGREES	COLD WATER
Fondant, Fudge	234 - 238°	Soft Ball
Divinity, Caramels	245 - 248°	Firm Ball
Taffy	265 - 270°	Hard Ball
Butterscotch	275 - 280°	Light Crack
Peanut Brittle	285 - 290°	Hard Crack
Caramelized Sugar	310 - 321°	Caramelized

In using the cold water test, use a fresh cupful of cold water for each test. When testing, remove the candy from the fire and pour about ½ teaspoon of candy into the cold water. Pick the candy up in the fingers and roll into a ball if possible.

In the SOFT BALL TEST the candy will roll into a soft ball which quickly loses its shape when removed from the water.

In the FIRM BALL TEST the candy will roll into a firm but not hard ball. It will flatten out a few minutes after being removed from water.

In the HARD BALL TEST the candy will roll into a hard ball which has lost almost all plasticity and will roll around on a plate on removal from the water.

In the LIGHT CRACK TEST the candy will form brittle threads which will soften on removal from the water.

In the HARD CRACK TEST the candy will form brittle threads in the water which will remain brittle after being removed from the water.

In CARAMELIZING, the sugar first melts then becomes a golden brown. It will form a hard brittle ball in cold water.

MISCELLANEOUS

A BANQUET FOR LIFE

This banquet has several courses, each of which are an important part of the meal. It takes practice to get it right. You have to have the best ingredients. The service is exquisite. The table is set with love, beauty, and order.

Ingredients: A man and a woman - each strong, each courageous, each honest, each with their own defined personalities, each independent, each with their own lofty goals and aspirations. They are matched intellectually, emotionally, and spiritually. The selection of ingredients is a most serious enterprise. The success of the banquet depends on the initial chemistry of well-chosen ingredients.

The appetizer: Romance. This is the magic that brings the lovers together. The spark may be physical attraction, sense of humor, easy conversation, shared values, or common interests.

It takes patience to get to know someone. Love evolves as they each grow in awe of each other's gifts, talents, qualities, and values. It is admiration and respect that melts the heart and creates the anticipation of something even better and more wonderful to follow. Affection is not given freely until hearts have been won over and commitments made. Winning a heart takes time.

First course: Commitment. This banquet will only be served in all its magnificent courses only when full commitment is given. Anything less will seem like fast food. Love can't unfold without confidence and vulnerability. There are problems to solve, faults to be overcome, differences to be tolerated, and mistakes to be forgiven.

Love won't grow unless there is safety for growth and change, for honesty and individuality. Commitment and trust allow love to grow in spite of differences.

Commitment means being loyal and faithful to your loved one. There are parts of your life that will only be shared with your loved one. Care is taken to prevent other loyalties or affections from taking your loved one from his or her rightful place in your heart.

Second course: Acceptance. Only the best of feelings will make this banquet special. The care and concern for each other's feelings is shown by tone of voice, patient listening, joyful greetings, and an understanding heart. Good feelings are maintained by keeping hostility, criticism, and negativity to a minimum.

Out of love and respect, you choose not to retaliate or respond in kind when your loved one is out of sorts. You might be justified but the cost to the relationship is not worth it. You or your partner can be foolish, wrong or difficult and be loved anyway.

Each is imperfect. There will always be differences, sometimes painfully so. What you each need is a friend who keeps confidences, gives the benefit of the doubt, and overlooks errors.

Third course: Communications. There are times for loving confrontation, undertaken with great consideration and respect. The language used should be soft and gentle, yet firm and resolute. Truth needs to be spoken, problems solved, differences worked out. Speak politely and gently. Give your partner's opinions respect and consideration.

Listen with your heart. Listen to understand. Suspend your own opinions, judgments, arguments, and solutions so you can hear what the other is saying. Listening is a way of caring, a powerful way of showing love.

Share intimate thoughts and feelings, the joys and struggles of the heart. Listen to the soul's cry when hardship, hurt or loss crosses your path.

Main course: Love. Dare to love. Be the first to love. Love creates love. Put your loved one ahead of yourself. Consistently. Daily. Serve and help one another. Make life less difficult for each other.

This happens with daily acts of love and consideration, soothing and comforting, encouragement and appreciation, smiles and warm words, kindness and thoughtfulness, sharing and giving. Needs are seen, anticipated and met - sometimes before the need is expressed. Love needs to be expressed in surprising ways and at unexpected times as well as on special days and occasions.

Cherishing your loved one takes a commitment of time. Loving couples spend time together. They enjoy one another's company. They are playful and have fun together. This meal tastes best when it is shared. Make wonderful memories.

Love means planning and working for a better future. Working together for common goals and priorities creates a union. Love means being involved with each other's work and activities. Family goals, children, material comforts, and vacations are opportunities to come together in a special way. The same can be said for sharing spiritual beliefs and practices.

Children and the grandchildren enlarge your capacity to love. This love is not for you alone but extends outward from family to friends and to the stranger along the way.

Dessert: Romance and passion. These are all the surprising ways to make you loved one feel cherished and special. These are thoughtful surprises, gifts, and remembrances. The extra effort is well worth the price.

Non-sexual affection, hugs, and touch are freely exchanged. The great moments of sexual passion and desire occur in a context of daily love and consideration. Coming together to enjoy physical intimacy is a fitting description for the dessert in a satisfying banquet.

Enjoy the banquet. It is well worth the work and sacrifice you put into it.
Dr. Val Farmer, AgriTalk Psychologist

CARAMEL TOPPING FOR ROLLS

½ c. white sugar
1 c. brown sugar
½ tsp. cinnamon

1 c. vanilla ice cream
1 c. margarine
2 Tbsp. white corn syrup

Combine in saucepan, stirring constantly. Bring to a boil and cook for 1 minute. Pour into a greased 9x13 inch pan. I use the frozen bread rolls or you can make your own dough. Place 12 roll slices on top of caramel. Let rise. Place foil over the top and bake at 350° for 30 to 35 minutes. Remove foil during last 5 minutes of baking. Let cool 5 minutes and flip over onto cookie sheet.

Peg Fast, South Dakota

WHITE FLUFFY ICING

¾ c. sugar
2 Tbsp. water
2 egg whites
⅓ c. corn syrup

¼ tsp. cream of tartar
Few grains of salt
1 tsp. vanilla

Combine all ingredients in double boiler. Beat with electric mixer until mixture stands in soft peaks. Remove from heat and water. Spread on cake.

Norma Uitts, Kansas

STUFFED FRENCH TOAST

10 slices day-old bread, cubed   **1 (8 oz.) pkg. cream cheese, cubed**

Place ½ of cubed bread in a 9x13 inch pan. Cover with cubed cheese, then add remaining bread cubes over top.

In a bowl, blend:

8 eggs
2 c. milk

½ c. maple syrup

Pour this mixture over bread. Sprinkle ground cinnamon over top. Refrigerate overnight. Bake at 350° for 50 minutes. Serve with Cinnamon Cream Syrup.

Cinnamon Cream Syrup:

1 c. sugar
½ c. light corn syrup

½ c. water
½ to ¾ tsp. cinnamon

Boil over medium heat, stirring constantly, for 2 minutes. Remove from heat and cook 5 minutes. Add ½ cup evaporated milk and stir well.

This recipe is a delicious breakfast dish.

Darlene Arens, Iowa

POPSICLES

1 pkg. jello (any flavor)
1 pkg. Kool-Aid (any flavor)

1 c. sugar

Combine preceding ingredients and dissolve in 2 cups hot water. Stir well. Add 2 cups cold water and stir. Pour into popsicle trays and freeze. Better than bought kind.

Grace Rasmussen, Minnesota

PRIZE WINNING CUSTARD

4 eggs, slightly beaten
½ c. sugar
2¾ c. scalded milk
½ tsp. nutmeg

¼ tsp. salt
½ tsp. maple flavoring
1 tsp. vanilla flavoring

Put into 1½ quart casserole and set in a pan of water. Cook for 50 minutes at 350°.

Art Gritton, Kansas

HONEYMOON SALAD

"Lettuce alone."

Lucille Jardon, Iowa

SHAMPOO

Shave 1 bar Kirk's hard-water castile soap in a pan. Add 1 pint warm water; stir and heat. Cover and simmer until mixture is a clear liquid. Fill jars with ⅓ concentrate and ⅔ water. Makes a lot for $.50.

This recipe dates back to before the year 1980.

Luella Suhr, Iowa

DEVILED EGGS

6 eggs
¼ c. Miracle Whip
¼ tsp. salt

Pepper
2 tsp. prepared mustard
1 Tbsp. chopped onion

Bring a large pan of water to boiling. Add 6 room temperature eggs. Cover. Turn off the stove. Let them set in the pan for 30 minutes. Pour cold water over them and shell them. Remove the egg yolks and mash them. Combine with ¼ cup Miracle Whip, ¼ teaspoon salt, pepper, 2 teaspoons prepared mustard, and 1 tablespoon chopped onion. May add crisp bacon bits and/or pimentos. Mix. Scoop into the egg whites.

Dorothy Earp, Texas

TASTY DRESSING

¼ c. honey
¼ c. mustard
¼ c. vinegar

¼ c. oil
⅛ tsp. your favorite seasoning

Mix well. Pour over lettuce and tomatoes or pour over grilled meat.

Margaret Horstman, Hopkinsville, Kentucky

PANCAKE SYRUP

1 c. sugar
1 c. syrup (light or dark)

1 c. sweet cream

Boil together for a few minutes or until it reaches a good boil.

Nellie Smith, Iowa

FUDGESICLES

3 to 4 Tbsp. instant gelatin
**   chocolate pudding**
2 Tbsp. sugar
1 egg

1 tsp. vanilla
1½ c. milk
Pinch of salt

Mix all ingredients and freeze.

Pauline Hopper, Illinois

124

HOMEMADE MUSTARD

1 c. dry mustard
1 c. flour
¼ tsp. salt

⅔ c. white sugar (or 1 c. if you like it milder)

Sift together the preceding 4 ingredients 2 or 3 times. (Batter will be lumpy if not sifted thoroughly.) Add ⅔ cup boiling hot water and mix thoroughly. Thin down with ⅔ cup white vinegar. Mix thoroughly. Pour into small jars and refrigerate. Keeps well.

Delicious on most any type of meats and sausages, except for fish or poultry.

P.S. Also good mixing ketchup and mustard together on your plate for another taste.

Orlene Renner Schaper, North Dakota

FAIRY CUSTARD

⅔ c. coconut
1⅓ c. scalded milk
2 eggs
⅛ tsp. salt

2 Tbsp. sugar
½ tsp. vanilla
10 marshmallows, halved

Place half the coconut in a greased dish; cover with marshmallows and remaining coconut. Beat eggs; add sugar, salt, milk, and vanilla. Pour into baking dish; set in pan of hot water. Bake for 1 hour at 325°. Yield: 6 servings.

Jan Bell, Iowa

GRANDMA O'BRIEN'S HOMEMADE MUSTARD

2 Tbsp. flour
2 Tbsp. sugar
1 tsp. dry mustard

¼ tsp. turmeric
Salt and pepper to taste

Add vinegar to right consistency (about 2½ tablespoons).

Lana O'Brien, North Dakota

GRANDMA'S NOODLES

2 c. flour
3 egg yolks
1 egg

1 tsp. salt
¼ to ½ c. water

Measure flour into bowl; make a well in center and add egg yolks, whole egg, and salt. With hands, thoroughly mix egg into flour. Add water, 1 tablespoon at a time, mixing thoroughly after each addition. (Add only enough water to form dough into a ball.)

Turn dough onto well-floured cloth covered board; knead until smooth and elastic, about 10 minutes. Cover; let rest 10 minutes.

Divide dough into 4 equal parts. Roll dough, 1 part at a time, into paper thin rectangle, keeping remaining dough covered. Roll rectangle around rolling pin, slip out rolling pin. Cut dough crosswise into thin strips. Shake out strips and place on towel to dry, about 2 hours.

When dry, break dry strips into smaller pieces. Cook in 3 quarts salted water or broth, 12 to 15 minutes or until tender. Drain thoroughly. Makes about 6 cups.

Three yolks and 1 whole egg equals 1/2 cup.

Nellie E. Value, Iowa

CHICKEN MARINADE

1/4 c. soy sauce
1/4 c. cooking oil
1/4 c. red wine

1 Tbsp. ground ginger
1 clove garlic
2 Tbsp. molasses

Mix all ingredients. Marinate chicken in this overnight, then grill chicken.

Don Evans, California

BROWN SUGAR APPLESAUCE

6 large firm, juicy apples
3/4 c. light brown sugar
1 c. water

1/8 tsp. nutmeg
1/8 tsp. cinnamon

Scour the apples well as peels are to remain. Core and quarter them and place in saucepan with sugar and water. Bring to a full rolling boil, then reduce flame to cook slowly until tender and thick. Press through a colander or coarse sieve. Add spices and serve hot or cold.

Variation: Add a little grated California orange rind when serving with duck or goose.

Pauline Hopper, Illinois

BLUEBERRY-STUFFED "FRENCH TOAST"
(The Maples Inn)

12 slices homemade-type white
    bread, crusts discarded and the
    bread cut into 1 inch cubes
2 (8 oz.) pkg. cold cream cheese,
    cut into 1 inch cubes

1 c. blueberries, picked over and
    rinsed
12 large eggs
1/3 c. maple syrup
2 c. milk

For the sauce:

1 c. sugar
2 Tbsp. cornstarch
1 c. water

1 c. blueberries, picked over and
    rinsed
1 Tbsp. unsalted butter

Arrange half the bread cubes in a buttered 13x9 inch glass baking dish. Scatter the cream cheese over the bread and sprinkle the blueberries over the cream cheese. Arrange the remaining bread cubes over the blueberries.

In a large bowl, whisk together the eggs, the syrup, and the milk. Pour the egg mixture evenly over the bread mixture and chill the mixture, covered, overnight.

Bake the "French Toast," covered with foil, in the middle of a preheated 350°F. oven for 30 minutes. Remove the foil and bake the French Toast for 30 minutes more, or until it is puffed and golden.

Make the sauce: In a small saucepan, stir together the sugar, the cornstarch, and the water and cook the mixture over moderately high heat, stirring occasionally, for 5 minutes, or until it is thickened. Stir in the blueberries and simmer the mixture, stirring occasionally, for 10 minutes, or until the berries have burst. Add the butter and stir the sauce until the butter is melted. Serve the French toast with the sauce. Serves 6 to 8.

Mark and Lisa Vail, AgriTalk

YEAST PANCAKES OR WAFFLES

2 c. flour
1 pkg. dry yeast
2 Tbsp. sugar
1 tsp. salt
1/8 tsp. ginger

1/8 tsp. nutmeg
1 3/4 c. milk
1/4 c. warm water
1/4 c. vegetable oil
3 eggs

Mix yeast with 1 teaspoon of the sugar and dissolve in warm water. Combine the rest of the dry ingredients. In a microwave-safe bowl, heat milk and oil to warm. Add dry ingredients and beat on medium speed about 1 minute. Stir in yeast. Add eggs and beat 2 minutes at medium speed until smooth. Cover and let rise until bubbly and doubled in bulk (about 1 hour). Stir down batter and bake on a greased griddle. Makes 30 (4 inch) pancakes or 5 to 7 waffles.

Prepared batter can be refrigerated 24 hours. Stir down occasionally.

Rosemary Teel, Missouri

RANCH DRESSING

2 qt. mayonnaise
2 qt. buttermilk
4 tsp. parsley flakes
4 tsp. powdered onion

4 tsp. powdered garlic
4 tsp. MSG or Accent (I use MSG)
1 tsp. pepper

Mix well and store in the refrigerator.

This is not a main dish, but our students *use it* on lettuce, baked or mashed potatoes, pizza, raw vegetables, tacos, and I've even seen it used over *jello!!*

I cook at the Golva Public School - this is a favorite. (Cut the recipe in half for home use.)

Shirley Schulte, North Dakota

ESCALLOPED PINEAPPLE

2 (20 oz.) cans pineapple tidbits, drained well (save juice for another time)

4 eggs, beaten until light
1 3/4 c. sugar

Add gradually while beating until light and fluffy.

Add:

4 c. cubed bread
1/4 c. butter, melted

The drained pineapple

Pour into a buttered 2½ quart casserole and bake at 350° about 30 minutes or until set. Serves 8 to 10.

Helen Toms, Illinois

HOT CHOCOLATE SAUCE
(For ice cream)

1½ c. water
½ c. sugar
3 Tbsp. cocoa

1 Tbsp. cornstarch
½ c. cold water
A little salt

Boil sugar and water 1 minute. Mix cocoa, cornstarch, ½ cup water, and salt. Add to hot syrup. Boil till thickens. Add vanilla flavoring and serve hot over ice cream.

Gert Winter, Minnesota

SWEET DILL PICKLES

1 c. cold water
1 c. white vinegar

½ c. sugar
3 Tbsp. salt

Stir up cold. Put dill in jars; fill with pickles. Add brine. Seal and put jars in warm water. Let get hot until pickles change color, about ½ hour. Remove pickles from water.

Gert Winter, Minnesota

ELEPHANT STEW

1 elephant
Salt and pepper

Brown gravy
2 rabbits (optional)

Cut elephant into bite-size pieces. This may take 2 months. Cover with brown gravy and cook about 4 weeks over kerosene fire at 465°. This recipe serves about 3,800 people. If more are expected, add rabbits. Do this only if necessary as most people do not like to find hare in the stew. You will need a very large kettle to cook this in.

Grace Fisher, Missouri

Notes

Notes

INDEX OF RECIPES

DESERTS

MISCELLANEOUS

KITCHEN HINTS

If you've over-salted soup or vegetables, add cut raw potatoes and discard once they have cooked and absorbed the salt.

A teaspoon each of cider vinegar and sugar added to salty soup or vegetables will also remedy the situation.

If you've over-sweetened a dish, add salt.

A teaspoon of cider vinegar will take care of too-sweet vegetable or main dishes.

Pale gravy may be browned by adding a bit of instant coffee straight from the jar . . . no bitter taste, either.

If you will brown the flour well before adding to the liquid when making gravy, you will avoid pale or lumpy gravy.

A different way of browning flour is to put it in a custard cup placed beside meat in the oven. Once the meat is done, the flour will be nice and brown.

Thin gravy can be thickened by adding a mixture of flour or cornstarch and water, which has been mixed to a smooth paste, added gradually, stirring constantly, while bringing to a boil.

Lumpless gravy can be your triumph if you add a pinch of salt to the flour before mixing it with water.

A small amount of baking soda added to gravy will eliminate excess grease.

Drop a lettuce leaf into a pot of homemade soup to absorb excess grease from the top.

If time allows, the best method of removing fat is refrigeration until the fat hardens. If you put a piece of waxed paper over the top of the soup, etc. it can be peeled right off, along with the hardened fat.

Ice cubes will also eliminate the fat from soup and stew. Just drop a few into the pot and stir; the fat will cling to the cubes; discard the cubes before they melt. Or, wrap ice cubes in paper towel or cheesecloth and skim over the top.

If fresh vegetables are wilted or blemished, pick off the brown edges, sprinkle with cool water, wrap in paper towel and refrigerate for an hour or so.

Perk up soggy lettuce by adding lemon juice to a bowl of cold water and soak for an hour in the refrigerator.

Lettuce and celery keep longer if you store them in paper bags instead of cellophane.

To remove the core from a head of lettuce, hit the core end once against the counter sharply. The core will loosen and pull out easily.

Cream will whip faster and better if you'll first chill the cream, bowl, and beaters well.

Soupy whipped cream can be saved by adding an egg white, then chilling thoroughly. Re-beat for a fluffy surprise!

A few drops of lemon juice added to whipping cream helps it whip faster and better.

Cream whipped ahead of time will not separate if you add ¼ teaspoon unflavored gelatin per cup of cream.

A dampened and folded dish towel placed under the bowl in which you are whipping cream will keep the bowl from dancing all over the counter top.

Brown sugar won't harden if an apple slice is placed in the container.

But if your brown sugar is already brick-hard, put your cheese-grater to work and grate the amount you need.

KITCHEN HINTS

A slice of soft bread placed in the package of hardened brown sugar will soften it again in a couple of hours.

Potatoes will bake in a hurry if they are boiled in salted water for 10 minutes before popping into a very hot oven.

A leftover baked potato can be rebaked if you dip it in water and bake in a 350° oven for about 20 minutes.

A thin slice cut from each end of the potato will speed up baking time as well.

You'll shed less tears if you'll cut the root end off of the onion last.

No more tears when peeling onions if you place them in the deep freeze for four or five minutes first.

Scalding tomatoes, peaches, or pears in boiling water before peeling makes it easier on you and the fruit — skins slip right off.

Ripen green fruits by placing in a perforated plastic bag. The holes allow air movement, yet retain the odorless gas which fruits produce to promote ripening.

To hasten the ripening of garden tomatoes or avocados, put them in a brown paper bag, close the bag and leave at room temperature for a few days.

When pan frying always heat the pan before adding the butter or oil.

A little salt sprinkled into the frying pan will prevent spattering.

Meat loaf will not stick if you place a slice of bacon on the bottom of the pan.

Vinegar brought to a boil in a new frying pan will prevent foods from sticking.

Muffins will slide right out of tin pans if the hot pan is first placed on a wet towel.

No sticking to the pan when you're scalding milk if you'll first rinse the pan in cold water.

Add a cup of water to the bottom portion of the broiling pan before sliding into the oven, to absorb smoke and grease.

A few teaspoons of sugar and cinnamon slowly burned on top of the stove will hide unpleasant cooking odors and make your family think you've been baking all day!

A lump of butter or a few teaspoons of cooking oil added to water when boiling rice, noodles, or spaghetti will prevent boiling over.

Rubbing the inside of the cooking vessel with vegetable oil will also prevent noodles, spaghetti, and similar starches from boiling over.

A few drops of lemon juice added to simmering rice will keep the grains separate.

Grating a stick of butter softens it quickly.

Soften butter for spreading by inverting a small heated pan over the butter dish for a while.

A dip of the spoon or cup into hot water before measuring shortening or butter will cause the fat to slip out easily without sticking to the spoon.

Before measuring honey or other syrup, oil the cup with cooking oil and rinse in hot water.

Catsup will flow out of the bottle evenly if you will first insert a drinking straw, push it to the bottom of the bottle, and remove.

If you wet the dish on which the gelatin is to be unmolded, it can be moved around until centered.

KITCHEN HINTS

A dampened paper towel or terry cloth brushed downward on a cob of corn will remove every strand of corn silk.

An easy way to remove the kernels of sweet corn from the cob is to use a shoe horn. It's built just right for shearing off those kernels in a jiffy.

To determine whether an egg is fresh, immerse it in a pan of cool, salted water. If it sinks, it is fresh; if it rises to the surface, throw it away.

Fresh eggs' shells are rough and chalky; old eggs are smooth and shiny.

To determine whether an egg is hard-boiled, spin it. If it spins, it is hard-boiled; if it wobbles and will not spin it is raw.

Egg whites won't run while boiling or poaching if you'll add a little vinegar to the water.

Eggs will beat up fluffier if they are allowed to come to cool room temperature before beating.

For baking, it's best to use medium to large eggs; extra large eggs may cause cakes to fall when cooled.

Egg shells can be easily removed from hard-boiled eggs if they are quickly rinsed in cold water first.

For fluffier omelets, add a pinch of cornstarch before beating.

For a never fail, never weep meringue, add a teaspoon of cornstarch to the sugar before beating it into the egg whites.

Once your meringue is baked, cut it cleanly, using a knife coated with butter.

A meringue pie may be covered with waxed paper or plastic wrap with no fear of sticking, if you'll first grease the paper with oleo.

No "curly" bacon for breakfast when you dip it into cold water before frying.

Keep bacon slices from sticking together; roll the package into a tube shape and secure with rubber bands.

A quick way to separate frozen bacon: heat a spatula over a burner, slide it under each slice to separate it from the others.

Cheese won't harden if you'll butter the exposed edges before storing.

A cloth dampened with vinegar and wrapped around cheese will also prevent drying out.

Thaw fish in milk. The milk draws out the frozen taste and provides a fresh-caught flavor.

When browning any piece of meat, the job will be done more quickly and effectively if the meat is very dry and the fat is very hot.

You'll get more juice from a lemon if you'll first warm it slightly in the oven.

Popcorn will stay fresh and you will eliminate "old maids" if you store it in the freezer.

Running ice cold water over the kernels before popping will also eliminate "old maids".

After flouring chicken, chill for one hour. The coating adheres better during frying.

Empty salt cartons with spouts make dandy containers for bread crumbs. A funnel is used for getting the crumbs into the carton.

A sack of lumpy sugar won't be if you place it in the refrigerator for 24 hours.

CLEANUPS

Fill blender part way with hot water; add a drop of detergent; cover and turn it on for a few seconds. Rinse and drain dry.

Loosen grime from can openers by brushing with an old toothbrush. To clean blades, run a paper towel through the cutting process.

Don't panic if you accidentally scorch the inside of your favorite saucepan. Just fill the pan halfway with water and add ¼ cup baking soda. Boil awhile until the burned portions loosen and float to the top.

A jar lid or a couple of marbles in the bottom half of a double-boiler will rattle when the water gets low and warn you to add more before the pan scorches or burns.

To remove lime deposits from teakettles, fill with equal parts vinegar and water. Bring to a boil and allow to stand overnight.

Before washing fine china and crystal, place a towel in the bottom of the sink to act as a cushion.

To remove coffee or tea stains and cigarette burns from fine china, rub with a damp cloth dipped in baking soda.

To quickly remove food that is stuck to a casserole dish, fill with boiling water and 2 tablespoons of baking soda or salt.

To clear a sink or basin drain, pour ½ cup of baking soda followed by a cup of vinegar down the drain . . .let the mixture foam, then run hot water.

When a drain is clogged with grease, pour a cup of salt and a cup of baking soda followed by a kettle of boiling water.

Silver will gleam after a rubbing with damp baking soda on a soft cloth.

For a fast and simple clean-up of your hand grater, rub salad oil on the grater before using.

A toothbrush works great to clean lemon rind, cheese, onion, etc. out of the grater before washing it.

While baking fruit pies, does the juice runneth over? Shake salt into the spills. They'll burn to a crisp and can be easily scraped up with a spatula.

Grease splatters or other foods that have dried on the stove, burner rings, counter appliances, etc., may be removed by applying dry baking soda to the spots, then rubbing with a damp cloth. Rinse with clear water, dry and enjoy the like-new look.

CALORIE COUNTER

Almonds:
    roasted in oil, salted, 9-10 nuts 62
Apple butter, 1 tbsp. 33
Apple juice, canned or bottled, 1 cup 117
Apples:
    fresh, with skin, 1 average (2½'' diameter) 61
    dried, cooked, sweetened, ½ cup 157
    dried, cooked, unsweetened, ½ cup 100
Applesauce, canned, sweetened, ½ cup 116
Applesauce, canned, unsweetened, ½ cup 50
Apricot nectar, canned or bottled, 1 cup 143
Apricots:
    fresh, 3 average (12 per lb.) 55
    canned, 4 halves with 2 tbsp. heavy syrup 105
    canned, water pack, ½ cup with liquid 38
Asparagus:
    canned, drained, cut spears, ½ cup 25
    frozen, 6 spears 23
Avocados, 3⅛'' diameter 185

Bacon, fried, drained, 2 medium slices 86
Bacon, Canadian, fried, drained, 1 slice 58
Bagel, egg or water, 1 medium (3'' diameter) 165
Bamboo shoots, raw, cuts, ½ cup 21
Bananas, 1 average 118
Bean sprouts, soy, raw, ½ cup 24
Beans, baked, canned:
    with pork and tomato sauce, ½ cup 156
Beans, green or snap:
    fresh, boiled, drained, cuts or French style, ½ cup . . 16
    canned, with liquid, ½ cup 22
Beans, lima, immature seeds:
    boiled, drained, ½ cup 95
    canned, with liquid, ½ cup 88
Beans, pea, navy, or white, dry, cooked, ½ cup 112
Beans, red kidney, canned, with liquid, ½ cup 115
Beef, choice grade cuts (without bone):
    brisket, lean only, braised, 4 oz. 253
    chuck, arm, lean only, pot-roasted, 4 oz. 219
    club steak, lean only, broiled, 4 oz. 277
    flank steak, lean only, pot-roasted, 4 oz. 222
    ground, lean (10% fat), broiled, 4 oz. 248
    porterhouse steak, lean only, broiled, 4 oz. 254
    rib, lean only, roasted, 4 oz. 273
    round steak, lean only, broiled, 4 oz. 214
    rump, lean only, roasted, 4 oz. 236
    short plate, lean only, simmered, 4 oz. 253
    sirloin steak, double-bone, lean only, broiled, 4 oz. . 245
    sirloin steak, round-bone, lean only, broiled, 4 oz. . 235
    T-bone steak, lean only, broiled, 4 oz. 253
Beef, corned:
    boiled, medium-fat, 4 oz. 422
    canned, lean, 4 oz. 211
Beef and vegetable stew, canned, 4 oz. 90
Beets:
    boiled, drained, sliced, ½ cup 33
Blackberries:
    fresh, ½ cup 42
    canned, juice pack, ½ cup with liquid 68
Blueberries:
    fresh, ½ cup 45
    canned, water pack, ½ cup with liquid 47
Bologna, all meat, 4 oz. 315
Boysenberries:
    canned, water pack, ½ cup with liquid 45
    frozen, unsweetened, ½ cup 30
Braunschweiger (smoked liverwurst), 4 oz. 362
Brazil nuts (3 large nuts) 90
Bread, commercial:
    Boston brown, 1 slice 101
    cracked wheat, 1 slice, 20 per loaf 60
    French, 1 slice 44
    Italian, 1 slice 28

    pumpernickel, 1 slice 79
    raisin, 1 slice, 20 per loaf 60
    rye, light, 1 slice, 20 per loaf 56
    white, firm-crumb type, 1 slice, 20 per loaf 63
    whole wheat, firm-crumb type, 1 slice, 20 per loaf . . 56
Bread stuffing, mix, mixed with butter, water, ½ cup . 250
Broccoli:
    raw, 1 large spear 32
    boiled, drained, cut spears, ½ cup 20
Brussels sprouts boiled, drained ½ cup 28
Butter, 1 Tbsp. 100
Butter, whipped, 1 tbsp. 67

Cabbage:
    red, raw, chopped or shredded, ½ cup 14
    white, raw, chopped or shredded, ½ cup 11
Cake, mix, prepared as directed on package:
    angelfood, without icing, 3½-oz. serving 269
    coffee cake, 3½-oz. serving 322
    devil's food, with chocolate icing, 3½-oz. serving . . 369
    white, with chocolate icing, 3½-oz. serving 351
    yellow, with chocolate icing, 3½-oz. serving 365
Candies, 1-oz. serving:
    almonds, chocolate-covered 161
    butter mints, after dinner (Kraft) 106
    butterscotch 112
    cherries, dark chocolate-covered (Welch's) 115
    chocolate, milk 147
    chocolate, semi-sweet 144
    coconut, chocolate-covered 124
    fudge, chocolate, with nuts 121
    gum drops 98
    jelly beans 104
    licorice (Switzer) 101
    Life Savers, all flavors except mint 111
    Life Savers, mint 108
    mints, chocolate-covered 116
    marshmallows (Campfire) 100
    peanut brittle 119
    peanut cluster, chocolate-covered (Kraft) 151
    raisins, chocolate-covered 120
    toffee, chocolate (Kraft) 111
Cantaloupe, fresh, ½ melon, 5'' diameter 58
Carrots:
    raw, 1 average 21
    boiled, drained, diced, ½ cup 23
Catsup, tomato, bottled, 1 tbsp. 16
Cauliflower:
    raw, flowerbuds, sliced, ½ cup 12
    boiled, drained, flowerbuds, ½ cup 14
Celery, raw, 1 outer stalk (8'' long) 7
Cereals:
    All-bran, 1 cup 192
    bran, 100% (Nabisco), 1 cup 150
    bran flakes, 40%, 1 cup 106
    bran flakes with raisins, 1 cup 144
    corn flakes, 1 cup 97
    corn flakes, sugar coated, 1 cup 154
    Cream of Wheat, cooked, 1 cup 133
    farina, quick-cooking, cooked, 1 cup 105
    oat flakes, (Post), 1 cup 165
    oatmeal or rolled oats, cooked, 1 cup 132
    rice, puffed, 1 cup 60
    wheat flakes, 1 cup 106
    wheat, puffed, 1 cup 54
    wheat, puffed, presweetened, 1 cup 132
    wheat, shredded, 1 biscuit (2½'' x 2'' x 1¼'') . . . 89
Cheese:
    American, processed, 1 oz. 105
    blue or Roquefort type, 1 oz. 104
    brick, 1 oz. 105
    cheddar, domestic, 1 oz. 113
    cottage, creamed, small curd, ½ cup 112

CALORIE COUNTER

cream, 1 tbsp. 52
cream, whipped, 1 tbsp. 37
Gouda, 1 oz. 108
Monterey Jack, 1 oz. 103
Mozzarella, part-skim, 1 oz. . . . . : 85
Muenster, 1 oz. 100
Neufchatel (Borden's), 1 oz. 73
Old English, processed, 1 oz. 105
Parmesan, grated, 1 Tbsp. 23
pimiento, American, processed, 1 oz. 105
Provolone, 1 oz. 99
ricotta, moist, 1 oz. 45
Romano, 1 oz. 110
Roquefort, 1 oz. 105
Swiss, domestic, 1 oz. 104
Cheese food, American, processed, 1 oz. . . . 92
Cherries:
sweet, fresh, whole, ½ cup 41
Cherries, maraschino, bottled, 1 oz. with liquid 33
Chestnuts, fresh, 10 average 141
Chicken:
broiled, meat only, 4 oz. 154
roasted, dark meat, 4 oz., no skin 204
roasted, light meat, 4 oz., no skin 207
Chili, with beans, canned ½ cup 170
Chili, without beans, canned, ½ cup 255
Coconut:
dried, sweetened, shredded, ½ cup 258
Cod (meat only):
broiled, with butter, fillets, 4 oz. 192
frozen, fish sticks, breaded, 5 sticks, 4 oz. 276
Coffee, prepared, plain, 1 cup 2
Coleslaw, commercial, with mayonnaise, ½ cup 87
Cookies, commercial:
brownies, from mix, with nuts and water, 1 oz. 114
butter thins, 1 piece (2" diameter) 23
chocolate chip, 1 piece (2¼" diameter) 50
coconut bar, 1 oz. 140
fig bar, 1 average piece 50
gingersnaps, 1 piece (2" diameter) 29
graham cracker, plain, 1 piece (5" x 2½") 55
ladyfinger, 1 piece 40
macaroon, 1 piece (2¾" diameter) 91
oatmeal with raisins, 1 piece (2⅝" diameter) 59
peanut sandwich, 1 piece (1¾" diameter) 58
shortbread, 1 average piece 37
vanilla wafer, 1 piece (1¾" diameter) 19
Corn:
boiled, drained on cob, 1 ear (5" x 1¾") 70
boiled, drained, kernels, ½ cup 69
canned, cream style, ½ cup 105
Corn chips (Fritos), 1 oz. 166
Crackers:
bacon-flavor, 1 oz. 127
butter, round, 1 piece (1⅞" diameter) 15
cheese, round, 1 piece (1⅝" diameter) 17
Melba toast, white, regular, 1 piece 15
Rye-Krisp, 1 piece (1⅞" x 3½") 21
saltines, 1 piece 12
whole wheat, 1 piece 114
Cranberry juice cocktail, canned or bottled, 1 cup 164
Cranberry sauce, canned, strained, ½ cup 202
Cream:
half and half, ½ cup 162
sour, 1 tbsp. 26
whipping, light, ½ cup unwhipped 358
whipping, heavy, ½ cup, unwhipped 419
Cream substitute, non-dairy, dry, 1 tbsp. 33
Cucumber, with skin, 1 large (8¼" long) 45

Dates, domestic, 10 average 219
Duck, domestic, roasted, meat only, 4 oz. 352

Eclair, custard filled, with chocolate icing, 1 average . 239
Eggnog, 8% fat (Borden's), ½ cup 171
Eggplant, boiled, drained, diced, ½ cup 19
Eggs, chicken:
boiled or poached, 1 large egg 82
fried, with 1 tsp. butter, 1 large egg 99
scrambled, with 1 tsp. butter, 1 large egg . . . 111
Endive, raw, 10 small leaves 5
Escarole, raw, 1 large leaf 4

Fat, vegetable shortening, 1 tbsp. 111
Figs:
dried, 1 large fig (2" x 1") 57
Fish cakes, fried, frozen, reheated, 4 oz. 306
Flour:
all-purpose, sifted, 1 cup 419
buckwheat, dark, sifted, 1 cup 326
cake or pastry, sifted, 1 cup 349
rye, dark, unsifted, 1 cup 419
wheat, self-rising, sifted, 1 cup 405
Frankfurters, all-meat, 1 average (10 per lb.) . . . 133
Fruit cocktail, canned, water pack, ½ cup with liquid . . 46
Fruit, mixed, frozen, sweetened, 4 oz. 125

Gelatin dessert, flavored, prepared with water, ½ cup . 71
Gooseberries, fresh, ½ cup 30
Grape drink, canned, 1 cup 135
Grape juice, canned or bottled, 1 cup 167
Grapes:
fresh (Concord, Delaware, etc.), 10 18
fresh (Thompson seedless, etc.), 10 34
Grapefruit juice:
canned, sweetened, 1 cup 133
canned, unsweetened, 1 cup 101

Haddock, fried, breaded fillets, 4 oz. 187
Halibut, fillets, broiled with butter, 4 oz. 194
Halibut, frozen, steak, 4 oz. 254
Halibut, smoked, 4 oz. 254
Ham:
boiled, packaged, 4 oz. (about 4 slices) 266
fresh, medium-fat, roasted, 4 oz. 426
picnic, cured, medium-fat, roasted, 4 oz. . . . 368
canned, cured, lean only, roasted, 4 oz. . . . 241
canned, deviled, 4 oz. 398
Herring:
canned, plain, 4 oz. with liquid 236
pickled, Bismark-type, 4 oz. 253
smoked, hard, 4 oz. 340
Hickory nuts, shelled, 4 oz. 763
Honey, strained or extracted, 1 tbsp. 64
Honeydew melon:
fresh, 1 wedge (2" x 7") 49

Ice cream:
hardened, rich, 16% fat, ½ cup 165
soft-serve (frozen custard), ½ cup 167
Ice cream bar, chocolate coated, 3-oz. bar . . . 162
Ice cream cone, sugar 1 cone 37
Ice cream cone, waffle, 1 cone 19
Ice milk, hardened, 5.1% fat, ½ cup 100
Ice milk, soft-serve, 5.1% fat, ½ cup 133
Ice milk bar, chocolate coated, 3-oz. bar 144

Jams and preserves, all flavors, 1 tbsp. 54
Jellies, all flavors, 1 tbsp. 49

Kale:
fresh, leaves only, 4 oz. 80
fresh, with stems, boiled, drained, ½ cup . . . 16
Knockwurst, 1 link (4" x 1⅛" diameter) 189
Kumquats, fresh, 1 average 12

CALORIE COUNTER

Lamb, retail cuts:
chop, loin, lean only, broiled, 2.3 oz. with bone 122
leg, lean and fat, roasted, boneless, 4 oz. 317
shoulder, lean only, roasted, boneless, 4 oz. 233
Leeks, raw, 3 average 52
Lemon juice:
fresh, 1 tbsp. 4
Lemonade, frozen, diluted, 1 cup 107
Lemons, fresh, 1 average (2⅛" diameter) 20
Lentils, whole, cooked, 1 cup 212
Lettuce:
iceberg, 1 leaf (5" x 4½") 3
romaine, 3 leaves (8" long) 5
Limes, fresh, 1 average (2" diameter) 19
Liverwurst, fresh, 4 oz. 348
Lobster, cooked in shell, whole, 1 lb. 112
Lobster, cooked or canned, meat only, cubed, ½ cup . 69

Macadamia nuts, 6 average nuts 104
Macaroni, boiled, drained, ½ cup 96
Macaroni and cheese, canned, ½ cup 114
Mackerel, fresh or frozen, broiled with butter, 4 oz. . . 268
Mangos, whole, 1 average (1½ per lb.) 152
Margarine, salted or unsalted, 1 tbsp. 102
Marmalade, citrus flavors, 1 tbsp. 51
Milk, chocolate, canned, with skim milk, 1 cup 190
Milk, chocolate, canned, with whole milk, 1 cup ... 213
Milk, cow's:
whole, 3.5% fat, 1 cup 159
buttermilk, cultured, 1 cup 88
skim, 1 cup 88
skim, partially, 1 cup 145
canned, condensed, sweetened, 1 cup 982
canned, evaporated, unsweetened, 1 cup 345
dry, whole, 1 tbsp. dry form 35
dry, nonfat, instant, 1 envelope (3.2 oz.) 327
Milk, malted, beverage, 1 cup 244
Muffin, corn, mix, made with egg, milk, 1.4 oz. muffin 130
Mushrooms, raw, sliced, chopped or diced, ½ cup . . . 10
Mushrooms, canned, with liquid, ½ cup 21
Mustard greens, boiled, drained, ½ cup 16

Nectarines, fresh, 1 average (2½" diameter) 88
Noodles, chow-mein, canned, ½ cup 110
Noodles, egg, cooked, ½ cup 100

Oil, cooking or salad:
corn, safflower, sesame or soy, 1 tbsp. 120
olive or peanut, 1 tbsp. 119
Olives, pickled, canned or bottled:
green, 10 large (¾" diameter) 45
ripe, salt-cured, Greek style, 10 extra large 89
Onions, mature:
raw, 1 average (2½" diameter) 40
raw, chopped, 1 tbsp. 4
Orange juice:
fresh, California, Valencia, 1 cup 117
fresh, Florida, Valencia, 1 cup 112
canned, sweetened, 1 cup 130
canned, unsweetened, 1 cup 120
frozen, concentrate, unsweetened, diluted, 1 cup . 112
Oranges, fresh, 1 average 71

Pancakes, prepared from mix as directed on package:
plain and buttermilk, 4" diameter cake 61
buckwheat and other flours, 4" diameter cake 54
Papaya juice, canned, 1 cup 120
Papayas, fresh, whole, 1 papaya (3½" x 5⅛") 119
Peach nectar, canned, 1 cup 120
Peaches:
fresh, 1 average 38
canned, in juice, 2 peach halves with 2 tbsp. juice . . 45
dried, ½ cup 210

Peanut butter, commercial, 1 tbsp. 94
Peanuts:
roasted, in shell, 10 nuts 105
roasted, chopped, 1 tbsp. 52
Pear nectar, canned, 1 cup 130
Pears:
fresh, Bartlett, 1 pear (2½" diameter) 100
canned, in heavy syrup, 1 pear half and 2 tbsp. syrup 71
dried, ½ cup 241
Peas, green:
boiled, drained, ½ cup 57
Peas, split, cooked, ½ cup 115
Pecans:
shelled, 10 large nuts 62
chopped, 1 tbsp. 52
Peppers, hot, chili:
green, raw, seeded, 4 oz. 42
green, chili sauce, canned, ½ cup 25
red, chili sauce, canned, ½ cup 26
Peppers, sweet, green:
raw, fancy grade, 1 pepper (3" diameter) 36
Peppers, sweet, red:
raw, fancy grade, 1 pepper (3" diameter) 51
Perch, ocean, Atlantic, frozen, breaded, 4 oz. 382
Perch, white, raw, meat only, 4 oz. 134
Pickle relish:
hamburger (Heinz), 1 tbsp. 17
sweet, 1 tbsp. 21
Pickles, cucumber:
dill, 1 large (4" long) 15
sweet gherkins, 1 small (2½" long) 22
Pies, frozen:
apple, baked, 3⅛" arc (⅛ of 8" pie) 173
cherry, baked, 3⅛" arc (⅛ of 8" pie) 211
coconut custard, baked, 3⅛" arc (⅛ of 8" pie) 187
Pimientos, canned, drained, 1 average 10
Pineapple:
fresh, sliced, 1 slice (3½" diameter x ¾") 44
canned, heavy syrup, chunks or crushed, ½ cup ... 95
canned, water pack, tidbits, ½ cup with liquid 48
Pineapple juice, canned, unsweetened, 1 cup 138
Pistachio nuts, chopped, 1 tbsp. 53
Plums:
damson, fresh, whole, 10 plums (1" diameter) 66
canned, purple, 3 plums and 2¾ tbsp. liquid 110
Popcorn:
popped, plain, 1 cup 23
popped, with oil and salt added, 1 cup 41
Pork:
Boston butt, lean only, roasted, 4 oz. 279
chop, lean only, broiled, 4 oz. with bone 308
loin, lean only, roasted, 4 oz. 288
Potato chips, 10 chips (2" diameter) 114
Potato sticks, ½ cup 95
Potatoes, white:
baked, in skin, 1 long 145
boiled, in skin, 1 round 104
fried, ½ cup 228
frozen, hash brown, cooked, ½ cup 174
mashed, with milk and butter, ½ cup 99
Potatoes, sweet:
baked, in skin, 1 average 161
boiled, in skin, 1 average 172
boiled, in skin, mashed, ½ cup 146
candied, 1 piece (2½" long x 2") 176
Pretzels, commercial varieties:
rods, 1 pretzel (7½" long) 55
twisted, 3-ring, 10 pretzels 117
Prune juice, canned or bottled, 1 cup 197
Prunes, dried, medium-size, 1 average 16
Pumpkin, canned, ½ cup 41
Radishes, raw, whole, 10 medium 8
Raisins, seedless (½ cup) 210

CALORIE COUNTER

Raspberries:
  black, fresh, ½ cup 49
  red, fresh, ½ cup 35
  canned, black, water pack, 4 oz. with liquid 58
  canned, red, water pack, ½ cup with liquid 43
  frozen, red, sweetened, ½ cup 123
Rhubarb, cooked, sweetened, ½ cup 191
Rice, cooked (hot):
  brown, long grain, ½ cup 116
  white, long grain, ½ cup 112
  white, parboiled, long grain, ½ cup 93
Rolls and buns, commercial (ready to serve):
  frankfurther or hamburger, 1.4 oz. roll 119
  hard, rectangular, ⅞-oz. roll 78
  raisin, 1-oz. roll 78
  sweet, 1-oz. roll 89
  whole wheat, 1-oz. roll 73

Salad dressings, commercial:
  blue cheese, 1 tbsp. 76
  French, 1 tbsp. 66
  Italian, 1 tbsp. 83
  mayonnaise, 1 tbsp. 101
  Roquefort cheese, 1 tbsp. 76
  Russian, 1 tbsp. 74
  Thousand Island, 1 tbsp. 80
Salami:
  cooked, 1 slice (4" diameter) 68
  dry, 1 slice (3⅛" diameter) 45
Salmon, smoked, 4 oz. 200
Sauces:
  barbecue, 1 tbsp. 17
  soy, 1 tbsp. 12
  tartar, 1 tbsp. 74
  tomato, canned (Hunt's), ½ cup 35
Sauerkraut, canned, ½ cup with liquid 21
Sausages:
  polish, 2.7 oz. sausage (5⅜" long x 1" diameter) .. 231
  pork, cooked, 1 link (4" long x ⅞" diameter) 62
  pork, cooked, 1 patty (3⅞" diameter x ¼") 129
  pork and beef, chopped, 4 oz. 383
  Vienna, canned, 1 sausage (2" long) 38
Sherbet, orange, ½ cup 130
Shrimp:
  fresh, breaded, fried, 4 oz. 255
  canned, drained, 10 medium shrimp 37
Soft drinks:
  cola, 1 cup 96
  cream soda, 1 cup 105
  fruit flavored (citrus, cherry, grape, etc.), 1 cup ... 113
  root beer, 1 cup 100
  Seven-Up, 1 cup 97
Soup, canned, condensed, diluted with equal part water:
  asparagus, cream of, 1 cup 65
  beans with pork, 1 cup 168
  beef broth, bouillon or consomme, 1 cup 31
  beef noodle, 1 cup 67
  celery, cream of, 1 cup 86
  chicken consomme, 1 cup 22
  chicken, cream of, 1 cup 94
  chicken gumbo, 1 cup 55
  chicken noodle, 1 cup 62
  chicken vegetable, 1 cup 76
  chicken with rice, 1 cup 48
  clam chowder, Manhattan type, 1 cup 81
  minestrone, 1 cup 105
  mushroom, cream of, 1 cup 134
  onion, 1 cup 65
  pea, split, 1 cup 145
  tomato, 1 cup 88
  vegetable beef, 1 cup 78
  vegetarian vegetable, 1 cup 78

Spaghetti:
  plain, boiled 8-10 minutes, drained, ½ cup 96
  canned, in tomato sauce with cheese, ½ cup 95
  canned, with meatballs in tomato sauce, ½ cup ... 129
Spinach:
  boiled, drained, leaves, ½ cup 21
Squash, summer:
  scallop variety, boiled, drained, sliced, ½ cup 15
  yellow, boiled, drained, sliced, ½ cup 14
  zucchini, boiled, drained, sliced, ½ 11
Squash, winter:
  acorn, baked, ½ squash (4" diameter) 86
  acorn, boiled, mashed, ½ cup 42
  butternut, baked, mashed, ½ cup 70
  butternut, boiled, mashed, ½ cup 50
Strawberries:
  fresh, whole, ½ cup 28
  canned, water pack, ½ cup with liquid 27
Sugar, beet or cane:
  brown, ½ cup firm packed 411
  brown, 1 tbsp. firm packed 52
  granulated, ½ cup 385
  granulated, 1 tsp. 15
  powdered, unsifted, ½ cup 231
  powdered, stirred, 1 tbsp. 31
Sunflower seed kernels, in hull, ½ cup 129
Sunflower seed kernels, hulled, ½ cup 406
Syrups:
  chocolate, thin-type, 1 tbsp. 46
  corn, light or dark, 1 tbsp. 58
  maple, 1 tbsp. 50
  molasses, blackstrap, 1 tbsp. 43
  molasses, light, 1 tbsp. 50
  molasses, medium, 1 tbsp. 46
  sorghum, 1 tbsp. 53

Tangerines, fresh, 1 average (2⅜" diameter) 39
Tomato juice, canned or bottle, 1 cup 46
Tomato juice cocktail, canned or bottled, 1 cup ... 51
Tomato paste, canned, ½ cup 108
Tomato puree, canned ½ cup 49
Tomatoes, ripe:
  raw, whole, 1 average (about 2⅖" diameter) ... 20
  canned, ½ cup with liquid 26
Toppings: dessert:
  butterscotch, 1 tbsp. 52
  caramel, 1 tbsp. 72
  chocolate fudge, 1 tbsp. 62
  pineapple, 1 tbsp. 56
Tuna, canned:
  in oil, solid pack or chunk style, drained, ½ cup ... 158
  in water, all styles, with liquid, 4 oz. 144
Turkey:
  dark meat, roasted, 4 oz. 230
  light meat, roasted, 4 oz. 200
  canned, boned, ½ cup 207
Turnip greens:
  fresh, boiled in small amount water, drained, ½ cup . 15
Turnips, boiled, drained, cubed, ½ cup 18

Vegetable juice cocktail, canned, 1 cup 41
Vegetables, mixed, frozen, boiled, drained, ½ cup ... 58

Waffles, baked from mix:
  made with egg and milk, 1 round (7" diameter) ... 206
Walnuts, 10 large nuts 322
Watermelon, with rind, 1 wedge (4" x 8") 111
Wheat bran, commercially milled, 4 oz. 242
Wheat germ, toasted, 1 tbsp. 23

Yogurt, plain:
  partially skim milk, 8-oz. container 113
  whole milk, 8-oz. container 140

This Cookbook is a perfect gift for Holidays, Weddings, Anniversaries & Birthdays.

To order extra copies as gifts for your friends, please use Order Forms on reverse side of this page.

* * * * * * * * *

ORDER FORM

Use the order forms below for obtaining
additional copies of this cookbook.

Fill in Order Forms Below - Cut Out and Mail

You may order as many copies of our Cookbook as you wish for the regular price.
Mail to:

AgriTalk
P.O. Box 901505
Kansas City, MO 64190-1505

Please mail _____ copies of your Cookbook @ _____ each.

Mail books to:

Name _____

Address _____

City, State, Zip _____

You may order as many copies of our Cookbook as you wish for the regular price.
Mail to:

AgriTalk
P.O. Box 901505
Kansas City, MO 64190-1505

Please mail _____ copies of your Cookbook @ _____ each.

Mail books to:

Name _____

Address _____

City, State, Zip _____

AgriTalk 1-800-794-8250